The Mass Audience
Rediscovering the Dominant Model

LEA'S COMMUNICATION SERIES
Jennings Bryant/ Dolf Zillmann, General Editors

Selected titles include:

For a complete list of other titles in LEA's Communication Series, please
contact Lawrence Erlbaum Associates, Publishers.

The Mass Audience
Rediscovering the Dominant Model

by

James G. Webster
Northwestern University

Patricia F. Phalen
George Washington University

LEA LAWRENCE ERLBAUM ASSOCIATES, PUBLISHERS
1997 Mahwah, New Jersey

Lawrence Erlbaum Associates, Inc., Publishers
10 Industrial Avenue
Mahwah, NJ 07430

Cover design by Semadar Megged

Library of Congress Cataloging-in-Publication Data

Webster, James G.
  The mass audience : rediscovering the dominant model
/ James G. Webster & Patricia F. Phalen.
      p. cm.
  Includes bibliographical references and index.
  ISBN 0-8058-2304-2 (alk: paper). — ISBN 0-8058-
2305-0 (pbk. : alk. paper)
    1. Mass media—Audiences.   I. Phalen, Patricia F.
II. Title.
  P96.A83W43 1997
  302.23—dc20   96–23823
                                                    CIP

Books published by Lawrence Erlbaum Associates are printed
on acid-free paper, and their bindings are chosen for strength
and durability.

Printed in the United States of America
10 9 8 7 6 5 4 3 2

To my sons, Henry and Jonathan.

—JGW

Contents

About the Authors

James G. Webster is a Professor of Communication Studies and Associate Dean of Speech at Northwestern University. He is the co-author, with Lawrence W. Lichty of *Ratings Analysis: Theory and Practice* (1991). He has published many studies of mass audience behavior, communications policy, and the impact of new media. Among these are articles with Ting-Yu Wang and Gregory Newton, whose work appears in chapters 5 and 6 of this volume, respectively. He received his PhD from Indiana University.

Patricia F. Phalen is an Assistant Professor, School of Media and Public Affairs, George Washington University. Her research interests include the operation of media industries, audience studies, and communications policy. She has an MBA from Boston College and received her PhD from Northwestern University.

Preface

Audience theory has experienced something of a renaissance in recent years. Much of the renewed interest is attributable to students of popular culture who take a critical, often openly political, perspective on the meaning of "audience." For those of us who have worked in audience research for many years, this is both refreshing and, occasionally, aggravating. Critical scholars have argued persuasively for a more sympathetic view of ethnography as a way to understand the role of mass media in the lives of audience members. They have found fault with the assumptions and standard operating procedures of mainstream audience research. Most especially, they have objected to the practice of seeing the audience as a vast, faceless collection of atomized individuals. They have, in effect, challenged the very idea of a mass audience.

This strain of criticism has provided one important impetus for our book about the mass audience. In some ways, the mass audience concept is a victim of its own success. In business, this way of thinking is so deeply ingrained in everyday practice that alternative constructions of audience scarcely come to mind. Unfortunately, the leaders of mainstream audience research, who include many "lapsed" professors, are often too involved in the daily demands of their industry to ponder or publish an academic treatise on the subject. In practice, the mass audience has become simply a fact of life.

To their credit, critical scholars have pointed out that audiences are not naturally occurring "facts," but social creations. In that sense, they are what we make them. We would include this as one of the more refreshing insights of the new audience studies. Our aggravation comes from the rather narrow reading these same scholars have of the mass audience concept and its implications. It is often characterized as a tool for the repression and control of the audience, or it is inescapably bound with discredited notions of mass society. We believe that this criticism misses much of what is good and useful in thinking about the audience as a mass. This volume attempts to provide a more complete picture of the mass audience in both theory and practice.

Chapter 1 addresses some of the questions highlighted by critical scholarship. Where does the idea of a mass audience come from? What are the
implications of conceiving of the audience in this way? And why has the
concept proven to be so durable? We find that the central, defining feature
of the mass is exposure to media. We also conclude that although the idea
of mass audience does serve certain institutional interests, it has the counterintuitive potential to empower the audience as well.

A second impetus for this book is simply to codify what is known about
the behavior of the mass. In chapter 2, we summarize the ever-expanding
literature on audience behavior, drawing on diverse bodies of research and
theory in marketing, neoclassical economics, and social psychology. This
chapter builds on a series of earlier efforts (Webster, 1980; Webster & Lichty,
1991; Webster & Wakshlag, 1983), and represents the most expansive
treatment of this subject to date. We argue that mass behavior has its own
dynamic, and that it is best explained by reference to structural factors.

Without doubt, the phenomenon most responsible for sustaining the
mass audience concept is its role in creating the audience commodity.
Commercial media sell audiences. This idea has been a central tenet of
media economics for many decades and has become increasingly important
in critical scholarship as well. Chapter 3, which is based on research by
Phalen (1996), discusses the trade in audiences and examines the determinants of their economic value.

One of the benefits of conceiving of the audience as a mass is that it
becomes a more tractable thing. Over the years, we have learned a great
deal about how the mass behaves. Indeed, some have argued that it
demonstrates law-like regularities. Chapters 4, 5, and 6 take up specific
topics of longstanding interest to students of audience behavior—inheritance effects, repeat viewing, and television news audiences. Our purposes
with each of these chapters are threefold. First, we provide additional
substantive material about each subject. In doing so, we review such
enduring features of mass audience behavior as the duplication of viewing
law and double jeopardy effects. Second, we demonstrate different techniques for analyzing mass audience behavior. To accomplish this, we
review data first published by Webster (1985), Webster and Wang (1992),
and Webster and Newton (1988). Third, by working our way through
hypotheses and real data, we hope that the reader develops a deeper and
more nuanced sense of this type of research, its potential contributions, and
its limitations. We believe that, taken together, these chapters say much
about the stability of mass audience behavior and how it is shaped.

In chapter 7, we consider the new media environment and the future of
the mass audience. A recurring theme in this book is that media structures
shape the mass audience, so we begin with an analysis of how the new
media may, or may not, change the rules. We believe that certain features

of mass audience behavior, like fragmentation, will become even more pronounced in that environment. Efforts to deal with these features will affect, among other things, how the audience experiences the media, how the trade in audience plays out, and ownership patterns in media industries. This chapter is adapted from earlier work on the television audience (Webster, 1986, 1989) and represents our most comprehensive statement about the future of the mass audience.

In chapter 8, we assess the place of the mass audience in media theory. Although it is the most common way for media practitioners to think about audiences, the mass audience is curiously marginalized in much of media theory. We review how this notion of audience is, or could be, applied in major areas of scholarship including media effects, cultural studies, and media policy.

We are indebted to many people for making this book possible. We would like to thank Jennings Bryant, Steve Wildman, Patricia Conley, and James Ettema for their ideas, advice, and critiques. We are also grateful to the National Association of Broadcasters, Nielsen Media Research, Arbitron, and Spot Quotations and Data for giving us access to audience information and pricing estimates.

Most especially, we are indebted to previous co-authors who have made substantial contributions to this work along the way. They include Jack Wakshlag, Head of Research at the WB Network; Lawrence Lichty, Professor of Radio/TV/Film at Northwestern; Gregory Newton, doctoral student at Indiana University; and Ting-Yu Wang, a recently minted PhD at Northwestern University. Much of what is good about this book we owe to them. Any errors or inadequacies are our responsibility.

Chapter 1

The Concept of Mass Audience

The audience is essential to our understanding of the media. It is the public in whose name programs are made and laws are passed. It is the commodity that supports commercial broadcasting. It is the arena in which the effects of mass communications are played out. It is the place where the meanings and pleasures of media use are ultimately realized. The audience, in short, is the foundation of the media's economic and cultural power. Without it, the entire enterprise has very little purpose.

Not surprisingly, the idea of an audience is common to both academic theory and industry practice. As McQuail (1994) noted, "it is one of the few terms which can be shared without difficulty by media practitioners and theorists alike" (p. 283). Most often, the audience is conceptualized as a large, loosely connected mass on the receiving end of the media. This vision of the audience seems so obvious, so natural, that no others may even come to mind. But audiences are not natural things. They are "man-made." And in the case of the television audience, a good deal goes into the making. Where do our notions of the audience come from?

In English, the word *audience* first appeared in the 14th century. Its original usage implied a hearing, as in "giving an audience." Eventually, that definition expanded to include an "assembly of listeners." Not until the mid-19th century, however, did the word take on a more modern meaning by denoting the readers of a particular author or publication. With the advent of electronic media in the early 20th century, the word was easily adapted to include the far-flung listeners of radio and television (*Oxford English Dictionary*, 1989).

Etymologies aside, the practice of assembling to see a performance is at least as old as civilization itself. Even the earliest audiences reflected something of the social structures and technologies of their day. In that sense, they share an important attribute with contemporary audiences. Each is a product of human engineering. Unlike media audiences, the first audiences gathered at specific times and places and could be seen in their totality by the performers. Just as importantly, the spectators could see and hear one another. Those in attendance were undoubtedly aware of their

1

membership in a larger audience and would act accordingly. As Brockett (1968) noted of early Greek theater, "the audience expressed its opinions noisily and at times hissed actors off the stage. Tradition has it that Aeschylus once had to take refuge on the altar to escape the wrath of the spectators" (pp. 39–40).

The existence of a media audience is less self-evident, partly because our knowledge of that audience is less immediate. It is unseen, and its members largely unknown to one another. At times, the broadcast audience seems as immaterial as the airwaves that bind it together. Yet, it is as real as those who first gathered to hear the plays of Aeschylus. In fact, the idea of a mass audience is so potent that it has come to dominate other ways of seeing the audience. This chapter explores the history, meaning, and remarkable durability of the mass audience concept.

SETTING THE STAGE

The idea of a mass audience can be seen as the outgrowth of trends dating back to the Industrial Revolution. Urbanization, mass production, the spread of public education, and the rise of a middle class all played a role in bringing the mass audience into being. The more immediate causes were the growth of advertiser-supported media and the increasing popularity of statistical analysis as a way to study mass social phenomena. Both of these factors deserve some comment.

The Rise of Mass Media

The mass media emerged in the 19th century in close association with manufacturing. During that period, manufacturers perfected the means of mass production. Indeed, they were so successful that their output could sometimes flood the market. Buzzard (1990) explained:

> As manufacturing became more and more efficient, manufacturers became victims of their own success: they could now produce goods at a much faster rate than the jobber/retailer network could sell them. When they recognized the problem, manufacturers began to examine it with the same analytical attitude and skills which had worked so well on the assembly line. Their conclusion, in effect, was that advertising would be the key ingredient in effective marketing. (p. 3)

Promoting brand images and uniquely packaged products became popular strategies for managing demand. But manufacturers still needed efficient ways to reach customers with their message. As luck would have it, at about the same time a series of developments in press and paper technology enabled the first inexpensive, high-speed printing. This combination of the manufacturers' desire to reach the mass market, and the technical means to distribute messages cheaply gave powerful impetus to the growth of mass media (Beniger, 1986).

For their part, the newly literate masses seemed hungry for low cost publications, made cheaper still by the presence of advertising. In the 1830s, the *New York Sun* began selling newspapers on the street for a penny apiece. The penny press placed a premium on circulation and encouraged editors to pander to their readers. Although some papers resisted these pressures and relied instead on the upscale quality of their readership to attract advertisers, by the end of the century, even the conservative *Chicago Tribune* had lowered its newsstand price to a penny. Newspapers had become a mass medium dependent on circulation for profitability. By the end of World War I, readership reached its zenith, with daily circulation actually surpassing the total number of U.S. households (DeFleur & Ball-Rokeach, 1982).

The growth of commercial broadcasting was even more phenomenal. Marconi had developed the first "wireless" around the turn of the century. Although it was originally conceptualized as a point-to-point mode of communication, it spawned a growing number of hobbyists who simply enjoyed tuning in. In 1906, inventor Reginald Fessenden transmitted what some consider the first deliberate broadcast.

> He played the violin, sang, recited poetry, and played a phonograph record. Then, the electrical engineer promised to be back on the air again for New Year's Eve and asked anyone who had heard the broadcast to write him. Apparently he got a number of letters especially from radio operators astonished to hear more than Morse code on their headphones. (Webster & Lichty, 1991, p. 68)

In 1920, KDKA, a station owned by Westinghouse, began a regular schedule of broadcasts designed to encourage the sale of radio receivers. By year's end, the federal government had issued 30 licenses. Five years later, more than 500 stations were on the air (Lichty & Topping, 1975).

At first it seemed that the sale of receivers might cover the expense of broadcasting. In 1922 alone, 100,000 sets were sold (Head & Sterling, 1987). But advertising quickly took hold. One of the new stations in New York City, WEAF, was owned by AT&T. For the telephone company, which made a practice of leasing its facilities to others, it was a short step to toll broadcasting (Banning, 1946). In 1922, a real estate company paid WEAF $50 for 10 minutes of air time to extol the virtues of an apartment complex. The same factors that brought advertising to newspapers now brought it to broadcasting. Almost overnight, radio became an advertiser-supported medium, free to listeners and intent on increasing its circulation (Spaulding, 1963). When television began growing in the 1940s, it simply followed suit.

But the broadcast audience was different from newspaper readership. It was more expansive and abstract. Unlike print media, it reached every segment of society. It could, and often did, entertain the youngest of listeners. It imposed no formal requirements of literacy. It opened the door to a vast national audience. Broadcasting, it seemed, was the ideal advertising medium. As Galbraith (1967) later wrote,

> Coincidentally with rising mass incomes came first radio and then television. These, in their capacity to hold effortless interest, their accessibility over the entire cultural spectrum, and their independence of any educational qualification, were admirably suited to mass persuasion. Radio and more especially television have, in consequence, become the prime instruments for the management of consumer demand. (p. 208)

Statistical Thinking

The realization of a modern mass audience, however, required a concurrent change in how social phenomena were conceptualized. Porter (1986) called that change the *rise of statistical thinking*. By the late 18th century, those who studied society had discovered that most social events, when measured in the aggregate, demonstrated unseen and remarkably lawlike regularities. The total number of births, marriages, crimes, suicides, even the number of dead letters in the post office, revealed predictable patterns that could be captured in statistical summaries of the mass. These regularities were all the more remarkable because the individual events on which they were based were themselves the result of countless, idiosyncratic circumstances and decisions. The social order that emerged from chaos occasioned much comment. Kant (cited in Porter, 1986), for example, wrote "since the free will of man has obvious influence upon marriage, births, and deaths, they seem to be subject to no rule by which the number of them could be reckoned in advance. Yet the annual table of them in major countries prove that they occur according to laws" (p. 51).

Throughout the 1800s, the practice of using statistics to understand and manage increasingly complex societies gained adherents in science, business, and public administration. As Porter (1986) observed, "After the mid-nineteenth century, it became common to investigate collective phenomena using what came to be called the statistical method, the method of reasoning about events in large numbers without being troubled by the intractability of individuals" (p. 12). By the beginning of the 20th century, most of the tools of statistical analysis had been invented and the stage was set to study the mass media audience as a knowable entity in its own right.

This entity was far more malleable and predictable than any one of its constituent audience members.

THE MASS AUDIENCE CONCEPT TAKES HOLD

It is impossible to identify a precise moment when the idea of a mass audience took hold, but a confluence of factors in the 1930s, including methodological innovations in audience measurement, key developments in social theory, and the arrival of Paul Lazarsfeld in the United States, suggest that the concept finally crystallized during that decade.

Audience Measurement

Advertisers had an obvious, pragmatic interest in knowing the size of the audience for any advertising medium. The more people there were in attendance, the greater the reach would be of their advertising message. For newspapers, this information could be obtained in reports of circulation, although some publishers were notorious for inflating claims of readership. The accuracy of such information improved after 1914 when advertisers established the Audit Bureau of Circulation to verify readership (Beniger, 1986).

The ephemeral quality of broadcasting made it even harder to measure its audience. Early techniques for assessing radio listenership included counting the number of receivers sold in a given market or tallying the fan mail received by a particular program. These techniques had obvious drawbacks (Beville, 1988).

In the late 1920s, Archibald Crossley, a market researcher and well-known pollster, suggested to the Association of National Advertisers (ANA) that more accurate measurement of radio listenership might be obtained by using telephones to survey the audience. Crossley's first report, *The Advertiser Looks at Radio* was widely distributed, and ANA members quickly agreed to pay for more regular reports (Webster & Lichty, 1991). In March 1930, Crossley initiated a new measurement service that he dubbed the Cooperative Analysis of Broadcasting (CAB). The CAB eventually went out of business, but the demand for audience measurement had been established. In the coming years, firms like A.C. Nielsen took on the task of providing estimates of audience size in radio and, eventually, television.

What came to be called *ratings research* coincided with similar advances in readership surveys. Marketing and advertising research began to take on the trappings of a profession. The U.S. Census Bureau developed the sampling theory needed for large-scale survey research, and textbooks codifying acceptable practice were published (Beniger, 1986). For those who studied the media audience, the 1930s were something of a watershed. As Chandon (1976) observed, studies of the press had "opened the field of media exposure by shifting the emphasis from counting the number of physical media units distributed to counting the number of individuals entering into contact with the media" (p. 3).

Certainly by the end of the decade, there was a well-established set of procedures that had the effect of defining the mass audience. Membership in the audience was to be a matter of exposure, of entering into contact with the media. Contact was to be assessed, in the aggregate, through the use of sample survey techniques and summarized in a variety of statistics. This provided a workable definition of the audience that was easily adaptable to the needs of advertiser-supported media.

The Mass In Social Theory

It would be a mistake however, to assume that the mass audience was nothing more than a device invented for the convenience of advertisers. Social theorists had a parallel set of interests. The dramatic, and often troubling, social changes of the 19th century, gave rise to a new science of sociology. Among the objects of its scrutiny were group behaviors that seemed ungoverned by law or social convention such as the action of crowds, fads, or other mass movements. These topics of interest eventually coalesced into a distinct field of study within sociology called *collective behavior.*

But, by the late 1930s, it became clear that a new sort of collective behavior had to be reckoned with. Blumer (1946) identified *the mass* as an increasingly important social entity, and described its characteristics as follows:

1. Its membership may come from all walks of life, and from all distinguishable social strata; it may include people of different class position, of different vocation, of different cultural attainment, and of different wealth.
2. The mass is an anonymous group, or more exactly, is composed of anonymous individuals.
3. There exists little interaction or exchange of experience between members of the mass. They are usually physically separated from one another, and, being anonymous, do not have the opportunity to mill as do the members of the crowd.
4. The mass is very loosely organized and is not able to act with the concertedness or unity that marks the crowd. (pp. 185–186)

The mass, then, is a heterogeneous collection of individuals who are separate from one another and act autonomously. That being the case, one is tempted to ask what defines it as a social formation? What makes it a thing that we can study?

A mass is unified by a common object of attention. It forms when a multitude of individuals select something as the focus of their interest. This act of choice-making defines individual membership in the mass and, in the aggregate, makes the mass a powerful social force. As Blumer (1946) noted, for each individual in the mass, the essential activities are

> primarily in the form of selections—such as the selection of a new dentifrice, a book, a play, a party platform, a new fashion, a philosophy, or a gospel—selections which are made in response to the vague impulses and feelings which are awakened by the object of mass interest. Mass behavior, even though a congeries of individual lines of action, may become of momentous significance. If these lines converge, the influence of the mass may be enormous, as is shown by the far-reaching effects on institutions ensuing from shifts in the selective interest of the mass. (p. 187)

Although these concerns are not unrelated to those of a merchandiser, the concept of a mass has broader applicability to the study of society. Furthermore, there is nothing in Blumer's definition of the mass that implies passivity or manipulation. To the contrary, the mass exercises power through independent, if unorganized, choice making.

The Lazarsfeld Tradition

The third factor that brought popular notions of the mass audience to fruition was the brand of communications research practiced by Paul Lazarsfeld beginning in the 1930s. Lazarsfeld has probably gotten more credit and/or blame than he deserves for founding the field of communication studies in the United States. What seems undeniable is that he exercised a significant influence on the way academics and media practitioners came to see audience research (Katz, 1987).

Lazarsfeld received a doctorate in applied mathematics from the University of Vienna in 1925 and began his career teaching statistics and psychology (Rogers, 1994). At the core of his interests then, and throughout his life, was the analysis of individual actions, be they voting behaviors or product purchases. As Czitrom (1982) noted, this approach to social science "proposed to organize psychology around the study of action, namely how people make choices between available alternatives. It differed from contemporary radical behaviorism in that it required some reference to individual consciousness in the explanation of why people act as they do" (p. 127).

In the early 1930s, Lazarsfeld received a Rockefeller scholarship that enabled him to establish a number of contacts in the United States. In 1935, with the rise of Nazi Germany, Lazarsfeld fled Europe. Not long after his arrival in the United States, the Rockefeller Foundation asked him to direct a project studying the still new medium of radio. Under the auspices of the Radio Research Project, Lazarsfeld oversaw a number of path-breaking studies of the radio audience. He also developed a close association with Frank Stanton, another young PhD who would become president of CBS. Lazarsfeld, an able administrator and promoter, parlayed his contacts with foundations and corporations into a more permanent research institute at Columbia University in the Bureau of Applied Social Research.

According to Schramm, the bureau was "the most influential communication research organization in the world!" (cited in Rogers, 1994, p. 264). It conducted a great many studies, often with corporate sponsorship, that later served as grist for academic books on media effects. Although one should be cautious not to oversimplify the bureau's research output, the Lazarsfeld tradition had a few distinguishing characteristics.

Lazarsfeld recognized the value of different research strategies, but most of his work used quantitative methods. He regarded himself as a toolmaker who could illuminate all manners of problems through the application of his research techniques. His work typically had an administrative purpose (Lazarsfeld, 1941). Rather than being critical of the established order, Lazarsfeld's research tended to have a pragmatic value or application for existing institutional interests. Finally, Lazarsfeld's whole approach to conceptualizing problems had what could be called a *marketing orientation*. According to Chaffee and Hochheimer (1985):

> The marketing orientation to research has been so intimately intertwined with much of communication research that it would seem inseparable to many scholars. . . . The focus of research, in this approach, is to differentiate factors characteristic of people, messages, and media to see where the most effective implementation of marketing techniques might be made. (p. 78)

Rogers (1994) made the point even more bluntly: "Why is market research close to mass communication research? Because one scholar founded both: Paul F. Lazarsfeld" (p. 289).

By the end of the decade, the combination of measurement technology, research practice, and theoretical predispositions had produced a rather distinctive way of conceiving of the audience. It was seen as a large, heterogeneous collection of people who were mostly unknown to each other. It was, in Blumer's term, a "mass." The shape of the mass audience was revealed by quantifying selected attributes of individual audience members and aggregating the results. Of central importance were the selections people made from available media offerings. Exposure was both the key concern of marketers and the essential, unifying characteristic of the mass. It defined the audience. Beyond that overriding interest in exposure, whatever approach could best describe how real people came into contact with the real media was fair game for behavioral scientists. We consider some of the perspectives used to explain mass audience behavior in chapter 2.

Just how big an audience had to be before it merited this kind of treatment was, and is, an open question. It must be of sufficient size that individual cases (e.g., the viewer, the family, the social network) recede in importance and the dynamic of a larger entity emerges. This is the essence of statistical thinking. Almost all media audiences, including those of eclectic magazines and books, would seem to qualify. Certainly, local ratings reports deal with audience segments of only a few thousand as if they were a mass. Although these are tiny audiences by the standards of national media, they are still large enough that most members of the audience are anonymous to one another, except perhaps as some "imagined community" (Anderson, 1991). Their actions, therefore, are uncoordinated, save for similarities of social circumstance and the unifying structure of the media themselves. These audiences are also large enough that they cannot be known in their totality. As a result, surveys based on random samples are the method of choice for empirical investigations of the mass.

This way of thinking about the audience had much to recommend it. It offered a pragmatic way to map media audiences that was relevant to industry, government, and social theorists. It allowed analysts to see the "lay of the land," if not every nook and cranny of audience experience. It was easily adaptable to different media systems. In a relatively short period of time, it became the most common, and for many, the only way of conceptualizing media audiences. Even beyond the United States, in countries less wedded to advertising and capitalism, the idea of a mass audience took hold (Mitchell & Blumler, 1994). It became the *dominant model* for studying the audience.

CRITICISMS OF THE MASS AUDIENCE CONCEPT

Perhaps because of its dominant position, the idea of a mass audience has attracted many critics. Taking stock of these criticisms deepens our understanding of the construct and its limitations. For the most part, faultfinding is of three sorts. Some criticize the concept for being obsolete. Others view it as a simplistic model of the audience, inadequate to address the central questions of communication research. Still others assail the concept as inextricably bound to self-serving, evil interests.

The Undifferentiated Mass

The first criticism derives from the proposition that "mass" implies an audience, undifferentiated by taste or social class, that consumes a standardized diet of popular culture (e.g., Escarpit, 1977). Television, by this measure, is the most massified of all media. Reacting against this construct, Cantor and Cantor (1986) stipulated "the assumption that there is a 'mass' audience for commercial television is false" (p. 215). Instead, they argued the audience is composed of "taste segments" that respond to diverse program types. This criticism of the mass audience becomes even more credible with the advent of new technologies. This change forces the question, how can there be a mass audience if there are no mass media? It would seem the mass audience concept is, if not false, at least obsolete.

Trends toward demassification of the media and its audience have been evident for some time (Maisel, 1973). Advertisers have certainly shown an increased interest in reaching narrowly targeted segments of the market. The media have responded with a proliferation of content designed to attract those market segments. For their part, the ratings services have introduced measurement technologies that allow them to report a bewildering array of audience demographics, further buttressing the process (Barnes & Thomson, 1994). McQuail (1994) described these changes as a shift "from mass to market" (p. 287).

It may be premature, however, to pronounce the mass audience dead and buried. Despite optimistic predictions about the future of new media, there appear to be real limits to audience demassification. Neuman (1991), for example, described a number of countervailing forces that are likely to limit media diversity and argued that, "both media habits and media economics . . . continue to involve strong incentives toward common-denominator mass-audience content" (p. 168). In a similar vein, Barwise and Ehrenberg (1988) questioned the likelihood of narrowcasting and concluded that "television audiences in the future will still have to be measured in the millions rather than thousands for programs to be viable" (p. 155).

But even if we foresee considerable demassification, it does not pose a fundamental challenge to the mass audience concept. As McQuail observed, the mass and the market have many characteristics in common. He enumerated the attributes of the market concept as follows:

It specifies the link between sender and receiver as a "calculative" act of buying or consumption. . . . Secondly, it ignores the internal relations of the set of consumers, since these are of little interest to service providers. Thirdly, it privileges social–economic criteria in characterizing audiences. Fourthly, the concept tends to limit attention to the act of consumption. . . . Fifthly, the view of the audience as market is inevitably a view "from the media." (pp. 287–288)

Such characteristics hardly suggest a revolutionary shift from one audience paradigm to another. At best, the idea of audience-as-market represents a slight adaptation of mass audience thinking.[1] Only if we insist on the restriction that mass audiences must be undifferentiated is there any distinction at all. That seems an unnecessary stricture that has scarcely applied in practice.

Newspaper publishers of the 19th century obviously catered to different social strata, and even early audience ratings noted demographic differences among listeners. Certainly the marketing orientation espoused by Lazarsfeld and adopted by industry encourages schemes of audience segmentation. Practitioners, in short, have always recognized the possibility that mass audiences could be differentiated. It is only when theorists deny that possibility that they turn the concept into a caricature.

The Social Character of the Audience

A second criticism of the mass audience is that it ignores the complex social relations that bind members of the audience together. By turning our attention from the social character of the audience we limit our ability to understand people's use of media and its effects. Freidson (1953) was among the first to voice this concern:

> The audience is only inaccurately termed a mass. We are told that the mass consists of individual members. When we look at a particular member of the audience we find that his actual experience is of a decidedly different quality than might be expected if he were a solitary member of the mass. We find that most individuals go to the movies in the company of another person and that family rather than solitary listening and watching tend to be characteristic of radio and television. The individual seems to experience those media frequently in an immediately sociable setting that cannot be characterized as anonymous or heterogeneous, with no interaction with other spectators, and no organized relationships among them. (p. 315)

Freidson agreed with Blumer that the defining act of audience membership was the selection of media, and that selections were therefore "the most important thing to explain" (p. 314). But he believed these were fundamentally social acts, causing him to reject Blumer's concept of the mass and its

---

[1] From time to time, throughout the rest of the book, we use the term *mass audience thinking*. This phrase is inspired by Porter's (1986) use of the term *statistical thinking*, of which mass audience thinking is a special case. Flowing directly from the mass audience concept, it is a way of seeing the audience that focuses attention on a limited number of characteristics, usually including some measure of exposure. It eschews interest in individual cases and social relations. Rather, it seeks a broadly based understanding of the population through quantification and aggregation.

methodological implications, "There is no justification for studying the audience as an aggregation of discrete individuals whose social experience is equalized and canceled out by allowing only the attributes of age, sex, socioeconomic status, and the like, to represent them" (p. 316).

The failure of the mass to reckon with social relations and group membership is at the heart of another criticism closely related to Freidson's. Ironically, this was made most effectively by Lazarsfeld, who had done so much to pioneer the methods of mass audience research. For him, the most important question was not one of media selection, but media effects.

According to Katz and Lazarsfeld (1955), early social theorists, whether they viewed mass media as an enlightening influence or a sinister threat to democracy, employed a simple-minded model of the audience:

> Their image, first of all, was of an atomistic mass of millions of readers, listeners, and movie-goers prepared to receive the Message; and secondly, they pictured every Message as a direct and powerful stimulus to action which would elicit immediate response. In short, the media of communication were looked upon as a new kind of unifying force—a simple kind of nervous system—reaching out to every eye and ear, in a society characterized by an amorphous social organization and a paucity of interpersonal relations. (p. 16)

Katz and Lazarsfeld (1955) found fault with this vision of mass society. Instead, they argued that media effects, especially short-term changes in opinions and attitudes, could only be understood with reference to a number of intervening variables, including interpersonal relations. These relations, it was said, promoted a *two-step flow* of communication, that limited direct effects.

Is the idea of a mass audience isomorphic with the mass society theory described by Katz and Lazarsfeld? Can we accept one while rejecting the other? Both conceive of a large, atomized audience attending to media messages. But the mass audience concept generally stops there. It does not deny the existence of social networks and may even consider them if they will illuminate patterns of exposure, but it generally ignores the impact or perceived meaning of messages. Mass society theory, on the other hand, goes beyond the usual concerns of audience researchers to posit a model of direct effects that has been variously labeled the *bullet theory*, or the *hypodermic model*. It is here that the construct becomes highly problematic. So much so, that contemporary scholars (e.g., Chaffee & Hochheimer, 1985; Pietila, 1994) voiced doubts that there were ever serious proponents of mass society theory. As Czitrom (1982) concluded, "the whole notion of a theory of mass society was something of an artificial and spurious construct, an intellectual strawman created by its opponents" (p. 136). Much like the caricature of the undifferentiated mass audience, mass society theory seems to have been a convenient fiction. At any rate, employing mass audience concepts need not imply acceptance of a simple bullet theory. One can easily reject mass society theory while embracing the idea of a mass audience.

The fact remains that mass audience thinking pays very little attention to the operation of social relations among audience members. This is a valid criticism, and it limits the range of research questions to which the concept can be profitably applied. Most notably, it can only take us part of the way to understanding media effects and provides us with scant information on the interpersonal factors that mediate exposure. It tells us little of how individuals are affected by the messages they encounter. Similarly, it offers only limited insights into how people use the media as a social resource or what that use means to them (e.g., Lull, 1980; Morley, 1986). To the extent that these are the central questions of media studies, the idea of a mass audience is of limited utility.

Who Represents the Audience?

At the outset we noted that media audiences are not natural things whose features are plain to see. Although there are surely real human beings out there who comprise the actual audience, we only know the audience by observing it through some sort of lens.[2] Depending on our vantage point, our eyes are drawn to certain characteristics while others drop from sight. In this sense, the mass audience concept tends to reduce the object of its focus to a statistical abstraction. The fact that audiences can be seen in different ways has caused some critics to question who controls the representation of audiences and what they accomplish in the process.

In its most benign form, this criticism simply acknowledges that audience measurement cannot quantify everything. Decisions have to be made about what is studied and trade-offs inevitably result. As Miller (1994) observed:

> All audience surveys, no matter how costly, limit to some degree the scope and detail of measurement of media content, audience response, and audience characteristics measurement. The nature and extent of the limitations are determined in the marketplace, where client demands for information confront the realities of what can be done in a survey and at what cost. (p. 59)

---

[2] This discussion should make it clear that any reference to the audience, let alone the mass audience, is always something of a contrivance. It is a construct useful to the theorist and/or practitioner. At the same time, scholars of all stripes are tempted to refer to an "actual audience" that has a real existence independent of how we measure or theorize about it. Certainly the term *mass audience* is often used as if it were a real, self-defining, entity—a simple collective noun. It is sometimes hard to know the difference between the construct and the real thing. We ask the reader's indulgence if we occasionally refer to the mass audience as the latter.

This is the kind of concern that one is most likely to encounter in the media industry itself. The issues raised are generally cast as technical questions of definition or method (e.g., what is the appropriate way to measure and report the audience for new technologies, or how does one improve the representativeness of samples?).

Although these concerns may sound arcane, the definitions of audience that are ultimately adopted can have a significant effect on the evolution of media markets (Barnes & Thomson, 1994). This has lead some critics to take a jaundiced view of commercial audience measurement. Rather than being a good faith effort to discover the truth about audiences, ratings are seen as products manufactured in response to market demand. As Meehan (1993) wrote:

> Since every measurement technique will err in some direction, the selection of technique becomes a matter of corporate strategy. After assessing the strategies of the rival rater, the relative strength of advertisers and networks, and the rivalries between networks, a rating firm selects its measurement technique carefully, using that selection to place itself strategically in the market. (p. 387)

This criticism goes beyond trade-offs earnestly made, and implies a systematic difference between commercial representations of the mass audience and the reality of the actual audience.

A variation of this criticism, more typically heard in academic circles, views the whole business of audience measurement as inescapably tied to a particular set of institutional interests. Ang (1991), for example, argued:

> Audience measurement is not just an innocent way of quantifying television's reach. The very act of head counting, which is the most basic operation of ratings production, is a very specific discursive intervention that results in moulding the "television audience" into a quantifiable aggregate object. Ratings discourse transforms the audience from a notion that loosely represents an unknown and unseen reality, a *terra incognita*, into a known and knowable taxonomic category, a discrete entity that can be empirically described in numerical terms. The audience commodity is thus a symbolic object which is constructed by, and is not pre-existent to the discursive procedures of audience measurement. It is this symbolic object—"television audience" as it is constructed in and through ratings discourse—that is the target of the television industry's practices, advertisers and broadcasters alike. (p. 56)

Viewed in this light, the whole *raison d'être* of mass audience thinking—turning the audience into a more tractable, knowable thing—is politically suspect. It is an unnatural construction of the audience imposed by outside forces to serve their own interests. Even audience surveys conducted by academics are not above suspicion, for as Ang (1989) noted elsewhere "historically, the hidden agenda of audience research, even when it presents itself as pure and objective, has all too often been its commercial or political usefulness" (p. 104).

Taken to the extreme, this line of criticism would have us believe that the mass audience concept and its associated measurement techniques are tools for the colonization and repression of the audience. The most chilling image of this disciplinary technology is the *Panopticon*. Originally cited by Foucault (1977), and subsequently taken as a metaphor for audience research (Ang, 1991) and public opinion polls (Herbst, 1993), the Panopticon was a prison design wherein a central guard tower looked out over an encircling ring of prison cells. The guard could observe every prisoner without being seen. The prisoners could neither see the guard nor one another. The cells were "like so many cages, so many small theatres in which each actor is alone, perfectly individualized and constantly visible" (Foucault, 1977, p. 200). According to Herbst (1993), this was a subtle but effective method of control, not unlike the techniques of social science: "Early statisticians sought social control through the observation of the body. Yet this was not an obvious application of power. It was power gained through knowledge, and the ability to watch and to count" (p. 24).

There is a good deal of truth to all of these criticisms. No audience study, however well-funded, can fully represent the audience. When audience measurement is done by commercial interests, their output is tailored to meet their clients' needs (Hurwitz, 1983). This can produce certain distortions, although it seems unlikely that ratings companies can drift too far from actual audiences as a common referent without losing business. It is true that the very idea of a mass audience is contrived. It is a construct, largely foreign to the audience itself, imposed by and for outside interests. As Williams (1961) said, "there are no masses, only ways of seeing people as masses" (p. 289).

Such critiques of the mass audience imply that there must be a better way to conceive of audiences, a more authentic way that speaks for the actual audience, a way that illuminates the "lived reality behind the ratings" (Jensen, 1987, p. 25). The most commonly cited alternative is to plumb the depths of audience experience with ethnography (e.g., Lindlof, 1991; Lull, 1990; Moores, 1993; Morley; 1992). This is indeed a welcome intellectual counterpoint to mass audience thinking. But, as even its proponents admit, it is of limited utility:

> What contribution can ethnographic understandings of the social world of actual audiences make to assess the dilemma? To put it bluntly: little in a direct sense at least. It cannot—and should not—give rise to prescriptive and legislative solutions to established policy problems, precisely because the

ironic thrust of ethnography fundamentally goes against the fixities of the
institutional point of view. (Ang, 1991, p. 166)

If this is the only method that gives a genuine voice to the audience, sadly,
it is quite feeble.

Fortunately, the audience speaks in different ways. What critics of the
mass audience concept seldom appreciate is the power that the construct
bestows on the audience. Aggregating individuals to create a mass may be
done at the behest of institutions, but it does not follow that this practice
inevitably fails to benefit audiences. In fact, we argue in the following
section that the mass audience concept empowers viewers in a way no other
model can.

THE DURABILITY OF THE MASS
AUDIENCE CONCEPT

Despite the criticisms and limitations, thinking of the audience as a mass
has been standard operating procedure for several decades, and we suspect
it will remain so for decades to come. The durability of the mass audience
concept is explained by its easy adaptability to a wide range of applications.
Many of these have been alluded to in preceding sections, but it is useful to
review them here in a more deliberate way. Broadly speaking, mass audience thinking has two seemingly contradictory uses: (a) as an instrument
of institutional control over the public, and (b) as the embodiment of
audience power.

The Means of Institutional Control

We have seen that some institutions treat the mass audience as a commodity. This is the most overt application of institutional control and, to many,
the most galling. By aggregating viewers into groups that interest advertisers, audiences are reconstituted as a thing of value. They can be bought and
sold, like corn futures or pork bellies. Even the language of this media
marketplace is dehumanizing, as people are transformed into "gross rating
points" and priced at some "cost per thousand" (Webster & Lichty, 1991).
The commodification of audiences is no small business. In the United States
alone, this is a multibillion dollar enterprise.

All this serves the interests of the institutions doing the buying and
selling. Marxist critics of western media conclude that such commodification constitutes exploitation of the masses because they are inadequately
compensated for their labor (e.g., Jhally & Livant, 1986; Smythe, 1981).
Whether viewers receive something of value in exchange for their attention,

or are simply dupes of the capitalist system is debatable. What is clear, however, is that conceiving of the audience as a mass makes this economic exchange possible.

The reason that audiences have value, of course, is that the attention of the mass offers an opportunity, real or imagined, to orchestrate media effects. By exposing people to their message, advertisers hope to sell their products, politicians hope to win votes, and social engineers hope to "serve" the public. Once again, this is an instance of institutions acting on the audience. Once again, the mass audience is the enabling concept.

The centrality of mass audience thinking in managing media effects is a bit ironic. As sociologists noted some time ago, the mass audience is a seriously flawed construct when it comes to theorizing about effects because it fails to account for selective perception or interpersonal influence. Its appeal is as much pragmatic as theoretical. Media planners have found that with a sufficient weight of exposure, media campaigns can reliably achieve lower level effects (e.g., creating awareness). These, in turn, create an environment where higher level effects (e.g., altering beliefs or actions) are possible. Thus, data on the mass audience offer a parsimonious way to delimit, if not determine, media effects. Even Katz and Lazarsfeld (1955) were quick to observe, "the mere fact of exposure itself is a major intervening variable in the mass communication process" (p. 22).

The utility of the mass audience concept in understanding or orchestrating social effects explains much of its popularity in situations where the economic value of the audience is not at issue. In the United States, for instance, the Federal Communications Commission has used data on the mass audience to determine when children are most likely to be in attendance in order to channel indecent language away from those times (Webster & Phalen, 1994). Certainly, many government owned systems rely on mass audience thinking to advance their own agendas—executing campaigns for the education, enlightenment, or indoctrination of the public. It would seem, then, that conceiving of the audience as a mass is just as valuable to the social reformer as the mass marketer. In all of these instances, no matter how self-serving or noble, the mass audience offers a means of institutional control.

The Embodiment of Audience Power

Because the idea of a mass audience empowers institutions, some critics are inclined to think it must strip individual viewers of what little power they have. Ellis, for example, wrote:

Broadcasting institutions are not concerned with "viewers," but they are with "audience." Viewers are individuals, people who use TV within their domestic and group social contexts. Viewers are the few people who ring in to the duty officer, or write to the broadcasters or to newspapers, expressing their opinions. Viewers record programmes on VCRs and use them later, pausing or replaying when attention wanders, shuttling forward when interest fades. Audiences, however, do not have these irritating characteristics. Audiences are bulk agglomerations created by statistical research. They have no voices and the most basic characteristics, they "belong" to income groups and are endowed with a few broad educational and cultural features. (cited in Ang, 1991, p. 37)

Such criticisms seriously mistake the power implications of creating an audience. Membership in an audience does not diminish an individual's ability to change channels or write letters to the editor. Far from taming viewers, aggregating individuals empowers them. It amplifies their voices and recasts them in a form to which institutions must respond. Ettema and Whitney (1994) referred to this as the creation of *institutionally effective audiences*. They said, "Actual receivers are not powerless but. . . they wield influence within the institution only when they have been constituted as some effective audience such as an identifiable and desirable market segment" (p. 11).

This kind of power is most evident in the way audiences hold sway over television programmers. Because selling audiences is the principal source of network revenue, attracting audiences is the central challenge of the organization. In a competitive environment this is especially difficult. Media executives have an understandable, if somewhat neurotic, obsession with winning an audience. Gitlin (1983), for example, quoted a television network programmer:

Because it's a mass audience—it's an unimaginably large audience—the audience tastes are so diffused and so general that you've got to be guessing. You can work off precedents about what's worked on television before. You can work off whatever smattering of sociological information you gleaned from whatever sources. You can let your personal judgments enter into it to some extent. . . [you can ask whether] this is something that people in Georgia or Nebraska will appreciate because they'll be able to translate it into their understanding. But you never really know. (pp. 22–23)

The constant need to fathom and respond to the tastes of the audience has led some industry pundits to characterize the system as a cultural democracy, wherein ratings data tally the votes. In 1988 Hugh Beville, the "dean" of broadcast audience research, wrote:

In a meaningful way, ratings are also an expression of democracy in action—viewers and listeners have free choice of a wide variety of free entertainment, news, and information. No other medium anywhere in the world can match the variety and quality of the total output of the programs that weather our ratings system to reach the American public. (p. 240)

The media's claim that they only give the people what they want strikes many students of popular cultural as self-serving propaganda (e.g., Ang, 1991; Carey & Kreiling, 1974). At the very least, it is an oversimplification. Peterson (1994), for example, noted how preconceived market segments fail to conform to the actual desires of the audience. Furthermore, as the following chapters demonstrate, audience formation is as much a matter of how the industry structures the media environment as it is a simple manifestation of viewer preferences. Nevertheless, the power of audiences to determine programming is considerable and is recognized as such in many formal economic theories (e.g., Owen & Wildman, 1992). Cantor (1994) concluded, "Because audiences can and do turn away from their television sets or do not buy tickets at the box office or books and magazines at the stand and in the stores, they do—in the aggregate—have influence on what is available to view and read" (p. 169).

Nor is the aggregation of individual choices significant only as a metric of commercial success or failure. Even noncommercial media are hard-pressed to justify their existence without an audience. Attendance constitutes a powerful standard against which all media offerings are judged. Simply put, if something is worthwhile, it will attract an audience. If it has no audience, how desirable can it be? This way of thinking about the audience was labeled the *marketplace model* by Webster and Phalen (1994). It offers a rationalization for much policymaking, especially in the United States. In fact, the marketplace interpretation of the public interest standard that has increasingly guided the federal government was put rather succinctly by Fowler and Brenner (1982), who argued that "the public's interest . . . defines the public interest" (p. 210). For better or worse, the actions of the mass audience are widely taken as confirmation of a program's value. Apart from any simple calculation of their commodity value, audiences seem to validate a program's existence.

In a broader sense, the actions of the mass audience are thought to reveal something about the nature of public tastes and popular culture. A simple comparison of the types of print media, music, or television programming that are most popular with young or old, Black or White, men or women, can hardly fail to invite some judgments about the culture. Of course, those bits of data are subject to different interpretations, but they offer an empirically grounded point of departure for studying the consumption of popular culture. This kind of exercise takes on a more theoretically substantive form in the work of Bourdieu (1984) and Gans (1974). Each creates audience aggregates to understand the workings of popular culture. Gans referred to this aggregate as a *taste public*:

> Taste cultures are not cohesive value systems, and taste publics are not organized groups; the former are aggregates of similar values and usually but not always similar content, and the latter are aggregates of people with usually but not always similar values making similar choices from the available offerings of culture. Moreover, they are analytic aggregates which are constructed by the social researcher, rather than real aggregates which perceive themselves as such. (pp. 69–70)

This is similar in many ways to mass audience thinking. It imposes a program of aggregation on the audience that recognizes people's choices as being of central theoretical significance. Although this kind of analysis could conceivably be adopted as an instrument of institutional control, in practice, it seems to be a method for giving voice to the cultural practices and preferences of the audience. This topic is discussed further in chapter 8.

Nowhere is the power of audience to mark the cultural significance of media offerings more evident than in the construction of *media events*. Sometimes events, like a championship game, are planned by the media. Sometimes, as with a natural disaster or assassination, they are not. Either way, these events gain much of their status by attracting an audience. And the bigger the audience, the more important they become. As Dayan and Katz (1992) observed:

> The live broadcasting of these television events attracts the *largest audiences in the history of the world*. Lest we be misunderstood, we are talking about audiences as large as 500 million people attending to the same stimulus at the same time, at the moment of emission. . . . The enormity of this audience, together with the awareness by all of its enormity, is awesome. (p. 14)

The presence of the mass audience not only authenticates the significance of the event, in a sense it becomes the event.

Because of its many applications, the place of the mass audience in media theory is sometimes hard to locate. In recent years, textbook writers and historians of the discipline have taken to identifying fairly discrete paradigms or models of communication (e.g., Black & Bryant, 1995; Katz, 1987; McQuail, 1994). Although labels and schemes of organization vary, we have yet to see a single paradigm into which the mass audience concept can be neatly pigeonholed. Mass audience thinking resonates across many models in communication, but none completely circumscribe it. McQuail's (1994) discussion of four models in communications illustrates the point.

The so-called *dominant paradigm*, draws on a "transmission model" wherein interest centers on "who says what to whom, through what channel and with what effect" (Lasswell, 1948, p. 84). Although mapping the mass audience goes a long way toward illuminating the media's potential impact by quantifying the "to whom" component of the equation, as we have seen, it stops short of the paradigm's ultimate concern with effects. Describing or modeling aggregated patterns of exposure, which practitioners have been quite successful at, is often an end in itself.

In some ways, the "publicity model" offers a better fit. According to McQuail (1994):

> Often the primary aim of mass media is neither to transmit particular information nor to unite a public in some expression of culture, belief or values, but simply to catch and hold visual or aural attention. In doing so, the media attain one direct economic goal, which is to gain audience revenue . . . and an indirect one, which is to sell (the probability of) audience attention to advertisers. (pp. 51–52)

Certainly, this captures many of the motivations of those who practice mass audience thinking, but it also falls short. As our brief discussion of media events suggests, audience attendence to media offerings, especially in large numbers, says something about our culture and the things we choose to celebrate. In that sense it implies a "ritual model" of communication.

At the very least, it would seem that the mass audience has little to do with the increasingly popular *critical paradigm* (Katz, 1987) and what McQuail labeled the "reception model" of communication. In this perspective, attention focuses on how members of the audience decode texts and make meaning of media consumption. But even this paradigm is not immune from mass audience concepts. As we argue in chapter 8, what an individual or an institution makes of a media message may be powerfully affected by what they presume to be the audience. Nor are the texts that a person constructs independent of their patterns of exposure.

The mass audience concept, then, is at once pervasive and theoretically ellusive. Far from being a static model, locked in history and dedicated to a narrow set of interests, it is a dynamic, adaptable construct capable of serving many masters. When we aggregate individuals, each of whom has little, if any power, we create something new and quite formidable. But the implications of this exercise are far from simple. Although the concept might be seen as a device for institutions to control the public, the mass audience is not so easily managed. In an ironic twist, the institutions that conspire to create the mass audience may find they have made something with a will of its own. In a manner reminiscent of the word's original meaning, the audience is positioned to provide a hearing. It has the power to accept what the supplicants offer, to turn them away, or simply let them wait and wonder. At the very least, we find that the mass audience concept is highly malleable and capable of fulfilling many purposes in theory and practice.

Chapter 2

Mass Audience
Behavior

Exposure to media defines the mass audience. Whenever large numbers of people watch television or read a newspaper, we have the beginnings of an audience. Out of these encounters we create a commodity, we define the reach of media campaigns, or we craft a yardstick that measures the popularity of media offerings. Given the centrality of exposure, the principle concern of practitioners, and a good many theorists, is explaining, predicting, and/or controlling how and when people come into contact with the media. In this chapter, we consider what is known about audience behavior and the many factors that influence it.

Before reviewing the various theories that offer an explanation of audience behavior, a few general observations are in order. At this point, it should go without saying that an important rationale for conceiving of the audience as a mass is to make it a more knowable thing. Many researchers have developed mathematical equations or models that allow us to predict audience behavior. Some have even gone so far as to posit laws of viewing behavior (see chapters 4 and 5). These laws, of course, do not bind each person to a code of conduct. Rather, they are statements that, in the aggregate, behavior is so predictable as to exhibit law-like tendencies. Conversely, this tradition of statistical thinking pays scant attention to any single case. In a very real sense, the mass takes on a life of its own, at some distance from the individuals who form it.

Although many forms of media attract a mass audience, our review and the studies that follow concentrate on electronic media. Radio and television are the quintessential makers of the mass audience. They are the most pervasive, the most accessible to the public, and, in the view of many, the most powerful of all media. For these reasons, contemporary research and theory on audiences is biased in the direction of electronic media, especially television. Our work shares that bias. When it seems appropriate we make references to other forms of media, but for the most part, television is the focus of our attention.

The behavior of the mass audience is typically conceptualized along one of two dimensions. The first, and perhaps more prevalent, offers a snapshot of the audience at a single point in time. It is the head count that is characteristic of much audience ratings research. The second dimension considers audience behavior over time. It requires the analyst to track individual audience members over some number of occasions and aggregate the results. Examples of the latter include studies of *audience flow* and analyses of media reach and frequency. Webster and Lichty (1991) referred to these dimensions as *gross* and *cumulative* measures of the audience, respectively. Together, they constitute the most common operationalizations of mass audience behavior. Specific examples of each are offered in chapters 4, 5, and 6.

The following review is drawn from a range of academic disciplines. As useful as scholarly research is, it would be a mistake to overlook whatever conventional wisdom can be gleaned from practitioners. Network programmers, media planners, and the like, have a kind of day-to-day intimacy with the audience. Although their experiences are often unreported, especially as empirical tests of academic theory, they have much to offer. As a result, we discuss working theories of the audience whenever they seem appropriate.

AUDIENCE FACTORS

The behavior of the mass audience can be located at the interface between individual audience members and the media. To explain how that interface takes shape and changes over time, we consider two broad categories of factors. These are, logically enough, *audience factors* and *media factors*. Each has a substantial effect on patterns of exposure. In each category, we make a further distinction between structural and individual determinants. Although the latter distinction is sometimes hard to make, it is intended to highlight differences in the levels of analysis. It also reflects traditional divisions in research and theory on media exposure. By *structural determinants*, we mean factors that are common to, or characteristic of, the mass. These macrolevel factors may be built on individual behaviors, but they reveal themselves only in the aggregate. *Individual determinants* are factors descriptive of a person or household. They are microlevel variables typically conceptualized as varying from person to person.

Structural Features of the Mass

The first structural audience factor that shapes exposure to radio and television is the size and location of *potential audiences*. Obviously, no medium can have an audience larger than the size of the relevant population. Sometimes the dimensions of the potential audience are easy to imagine, for example, the number of people living in the coverage area of a broadcast signal. Sometimes the relevant population is harder to conceptualize, as is the case with international markets or films released in different media over time (Wildman, 1994). Nevertheless, the population sets an upper bound on the audience for any content or program service. If the relevant population is small, so too will be the audience.

Recognizing the size of potential audiences has a powerful effect on the behavior of mass media organizations. Shifting population demographics often foretell the rise or fall of media that cater to those markets. In the United States, for example, the rapid growth of Latino populations has made Spanish language programming more viable than it was 20 years ago. According to Wildman (1994), as the size of the potential audience increases, profit maximizing firms are willing to invest more in the media products that compete for that audience. Among other things, this phenomenon is thought to explain why English language programs dominate international trade in film and video (Wildman & Siwek, 1988).

The second structural attribute of audiences, and one of the most powerful determinants of exposure to the electronic media, is *audience availability*. Although potential audiences set an absolute physical limit on audience sizes, our daily routines set a practical limit on how many people are likely to be using either radio or television at any point in time. It is widely believed that the number of people using a medium has little, if anything, to do with programming and almost everything to do with who is available. Most practitioners take the size of the available audience as given, just as they would the size of the population itself. In practice, the available audience is most often defined as the number of people using a medium at any point in time.

The idea that the total audience is determined by things other than programming is embedded in both the conventional wisdom of programmers and more formal theories of audience behavior. In 1971, Paul Klein, then a researcher at NBC, offered a tongue-in-cheek description of the television audience. Struck by the amazing predictability of audience size, Klein suggested that people turn the set on out of habit, without much advance thought about what they will watch. After the set is on, they simply choose the *least objectionable program* (LOP) from available offerings.

In effect, what Klein suggested was that audience behavior is a two-stage process wherein a decision to use the media precedes the selection of specific content. The tendency of people to turn on a set without regard to programming is often taken as evidence of a *passive audience*—although that label seems needlessly value-laden. The conceptual alternative, a thoroughly *active audience*, seems unrealistic. Such an audience would turn on a set whenever favorite programs were aired, and turn off a set when they were not. We know, however, that our daily schedules (e.g., work, sleep, etc.) effectively constrain when we turn sets on. We also know that many people will watch or listen to programming they are not thrilled with, rather than turn off their sets.

Of course, this is a broad generalization about audience behavior. It is not intended to rule out the possibility that people can be persuaded to turn on their sets by media content. Media events undoubtedly attract people to the television who would not otherwise watch. Nor does it mean that everyone is the same in their use of media. Activity levels can be conceptualized as varying over time or from person to person (Hearn, 1989; Hirsch, 1980; Levy & Windahl, 1984; Rubin, 1993). Even the same person might be choosy at one point and a "couch potato" the next. Overall, this two-stage process appears to explain audience behavior quite well, and has been adopted in many models of program choice (e.g., Gensch & Shaman, 1980; Owen & Wildman, 1992; Rust, Kamakura, & Alpert, 1992; Webster & Wakshlag, 1983).

Whatever the explanation, the size of the available audience, like other forms of mass behavior, is quite predictable. Three patterns are apparent: seasonal, daily, and hourly. Seasonal patterns of media use are clearly evident in television viewing behavior (Barnett, Chang, Fink, & Richards, 1991; Gensch & Shaman, 1980). Nationwide, television use is heaviest in the winter months of January and February. Nielsen reports that the average household has a set in use for almost 8 hours a day at this time of year. During the summer months, household usage drops to about 6½ hours. This shift seems to occur because viewers have more daylight in the summer, and pursue outdoor activities that take them away from the set. In the aggregate, this means the television audience is larger in the winter and smaller in the summer. Additionally, underneath these household-level data, different segments of the population exhibit unique patterns. For example, when school is not in session, daytime viewing among children and teenagers soars. The same vacation time phenomenon appears to account for seasonal differences in movie theater attendance (Vogel, 1994).

In broadcasting, audience size also varies by the day of the week. Nationwide, prime-time television audiences are higher on weekdays and Sunday, and lower on Fridays and Saturdays (Nielsen Media Research, 1993). The late-night audience (e.g., midnight) on Friday and Saturday, however, is larger than it is during the rest of the week. Once again, this seems to reflect a change in people's social activities on the weekends. Radio audiences also vary from weekdays to weekends, with smaller early morning audiences on Saturday and Sunday.

The most dramatic shifts in audience availability, however, occur on an hourly basis. It is here that the patterns of each day's life are most evident. Figure 2.1 offers a hypothetical depiction of audience availabilities throughout a typical workday. The figure is based on years of experience looking

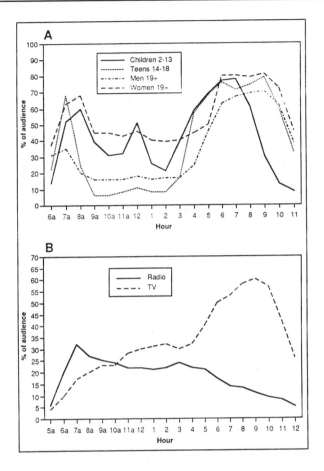

FIG. 2.1. Hypothetical audience availability and typical patterns of radio and television use. From Webster & Lichty, 1991.

at audience data from a variety of sources. The top graph, labeled A, shows when various segments of the audience are likely to be available to use electronic media. During school and business hours, availability is relatively limited, although it is worth noting that many people listen to the radio in their workplace. The bottom graph, labeled B, represents the variation in total audience size that results from these availabilities. Media use in the morning generally favors radio. In most markets, radio listening hits a peak around 7 a.m. or 8 a.m., as people commute to work. There is a less pronouced "blip" in the audience during the afternoon commute. In the industry, these periods are referred to as *drive time*. By midmorning, the television audience begins to exceed the radio audience. At roughly 5 p.m., when people arrive home from work, TVs go on and audience levels rise sharply. The total size of audience peaks between 9 p.m. and 10 p.m., which marks the height of prime time. At that point, a large majority of households are likely to have a television set in use.

In any given market, these hourly patterns of media use are remarkably stable. This is not to say they are written in stone. As more and more women enter the workforce, or as people begin to telecommute, patterns of availability may change. But, from one year to the next, this kind of aggregated audience behavior is highly predictable. In fact, it is bedrock on which media buyers and sellers build their estimates of future ratings (Webster & Lichty, 1991).

Audience availability is critical in evaluating the size of a program's audience. A rating during one part of the day might be quite acceptable, and during another, a disaster. For example, the broadcast networks have long vied for the early morning television audience with news programs like the *Today Show* and *Good Morning America*. The winner of these competitions will have an average rating of about 4 or 5, meaning that 4% or 5% of all television households have tuned in the program. During prime time, however, network shows with a rating twice that large will almost certainly be canceled (Atkin & Litman, 1986). In other words, the size of the available audience imposes certain expectations about how large an audience a program can capture at any one point in time.

Thus far, we considered availability only as a matter of gross audience size. One can also consider patterns of availability across time. For example, are certain segments of the population more consistently available than others? Do the people who watch television at 8 p.m. on one night watch again at the same time the following evening? These questions address cumulative behaviors. Here too, there are some fairly stable, if less well-known, patterns to report.

The first point to remember is that different people consume very different amounts of radio and television. The average American watches about 4 hours of television a day, and listens to the radio for roughly 3 hours. These, of course, are only averages. Some people use a medium much more than the average, others much less (Paik & Marzban, 1995). Indeed, about one fifth of all Americans watch nearly 12 hours a day whereas another one fifth average less than 30 minutes per day. A portion of this variation can be associated with the demographic characteristics of the audience. People 45 years old or older are known to use less radio and more television than the rest of the population. Slightly heavier than average television viewing is also associated with lower levels of income and education. These individual differences in media consumption are often explained in terms of availability. Older people are thought to watch more TV because they have more time on their hands and fewer activities that take them outside the home. In any event, individual differences in media use produce certain patterns of *audience overlap* that are not apparent in the gross measures of audience size just reviewed.

To understand this, imagine that half of all households watch TV one night, and that 50% of all sets are again in use the following night. To what extent are the people who watched TV one night watching again the following night? This is a question of audience overlap. One possibility is that the same 50% of the population is watching on both days. This would be the case if half the population always watched TV and the other half never watched. Such mass behavior seems highly unlikely. Another possibility is that everyone watches the same amount, and that his or her presence in the audience varies randomly from night to night. If that were the case, only 25% of the entire audience would have been watching TV on both evenings (i.e., 50% x 50% = 25%). In other words, audience overlap would be exactly proportional to the total audience. This outcome is also unlikely because we know that some people are relatively heavy users, and are therefore more apt to be in the audience on a day-to-day basis.

When comparisons of total audience overlap are actually made, the level of overlap does, in fact, exceed chance. According to Barwise and Ehrenberg (1988), observed levels of overlap tend to be one fifth higher than chance. In our example then, roughly 30% of the population could be expected to have been watching television on both evenings. Stated differently, 60% of the people who watched one night are watching again the following night. As it turns out, these patterns of overlap are stable even over more widely separated days.

One important exception to the Barwise-Ehrenberg one fifth rule of thumb applies when we look at audience overlap in adjacent time periods. If we consider audience consistency hour to hour, we find the same people are much more likely to be in the audience. For example, of the people who watch television at 7 p.m., about 70% to 80% will be watching at 8 p.m. on the same night. As hours become more widely separated, however, audience overlap drops to the more usual levels. We explore this phenomenon in greater detail in chapter 4.

Just as knowing the size of the available audience tempered our interpretation of ratings, an appreciation of audience overlap can inform our assessment of cumulative measurements. Among segments of the population that are heavy users of television, we should expect a relatively high frequency of exposure to programs and advertising. Similarly, if we are examining audience flow between programs that are scheduled back-to-back, we should expect higher levels of audience duplication than between programs that are scheduled days, or even hours apart. Table 2.1 provides a summary of how availability can affect patterns of mass audience behavior.

Thus far, our approach to explaining mass audience behavior has had almost nothing to say about people's preferences, or the appeals of different

TABLE 2.1
Patterns of Availability Affecting Mass Audience Behavior

Gross Behavior	Selected References
Seasonal Variation	Barnett et al. (1991)
	Gensch & Shaman (1980)
Daily Variation	Nielsen Media Research (1993)
	Webster & Lichty (1991)
Hourly Variation	Barwise & Ehrenberg (1988)
	Goodhardt et al. (1987)
	Nielsen Media Research (1993)
	Webster & Lichty (1991)
Cumulative Behavior	Selected References
Individual Variation	Barwise & Ehrenberg (1988)
	Paik & Marzban (1995)
	Nielsen Media Research (1993)
Total Audience Overlap	Barwise & Ehrenberg (1988)
	Webster (1985)

kinds of programming. Remember, however, audience behavior is best conceptualized as a two-stage process. Turning on a set may have little to do with specific content, but once a decision to use the media has been made, people's likes and dislikes, as well as a number of other contingencies, come into play. These are the microlevel determinants of audience behavior.

The Traits of Individuals

Several factors affect an individual's choice of media offerings. For both industry practitioners and theorists, the most important of these is, broadly speaking, people's preferences. Much of a programmer's skill in building an audience comes from an ability to judge what people will or will not like. *Program preferences* also figure prominently in many theories of program choice. Although each academic discipline employs a slightly different theoretical framework and vocabulary, the fundamental mechanism for explaining audience behavior is essentially the same. Therefore it seems appropriate to make some general observations about this mode of theorizing before reviewing more discrete bodies of work.

Preferences are conditions of mind that cannot be directly observed. Their invisibility is important because it means we can know of their existence only indirectly. Strict behaviorists are skeptical of such approaches, preferring instead to study only what can be seen. Many scholars, however, find ideas like preferences, attitudes, values, needs, tastes, and wants useful tools for understanding human behavior (Kim & Hunter, 1993). Certainly, we use these concepts in our everyday lives. But how can we really know a person's preferences? How do we even know such things exist?

Sometimes, we simply ask people what they like, but often we infer preferences from their behavior. The latter approach is taken by economists, as expressed in the axiom of *revealed preferences* (Mansfield, 1970). It is also common in psychological research on attitudes. Basically, there is an expectation that a person's attitudes will be consistent with his or her behavior. In fact, this assumption is inherent in the definition of *attitudes* as "predispositions to respond in a particular way toward a specified class of objects" (Rosenberg & Hovland, 1960, p. 1). This simple link between affect and action offers a powerful concept for explaining behavior that typifies the approaches cited here. Indeed, some researchers find the linkage so compelling that they use preference and choice interchangeably.

Marketing researchers and neoclassical economists share an interest in modeling program choice that illustrates this approach to audience theory. The former are interested in predicting ratings or crafting more effective media campaigns, the latter are generally concerned with testing the welfare implications of different industry structures. Either way, they make certain similar assumptions about program preferences and the role they play in audience behavior.

Peter Steiner is credited with the seminal work in this field of economics. Steiner (1952), and those who have extended his work (e.g., Owen & Wildman, 1992; Waterman, 1992), take the approach that a person's choice of programming is analogous to his or her choice of more conventional consumer products. Hence, older theories of product competition have served as the model for economic theories of program choice (see Hotelling, 1929). Under such theories, two important assumptions about the audience are made. The first has to do with the "free good" nature of the programs and its implications. The second involves the structure of viewer preferences.

The assumption that programs are free to viewers is of considerable importance. In the process of stating the assumption, the opportunity cost of audience time, and the increased costs of advertised products are explicitly ignored (Owen & Wildman, 1992). But what the free good assumption also implies is a direct causal link between preference and choice that sometimes eludes notice. Recall that under these models, programs have been likened to consumer goods. In the absence of any charge for the product, it seems logical that the only thing left to explain audience choice is preference. Some models of choice are clear about the linkage (e.g., Bowman & Farley, 1972). Others simply take program choice as a measure of preference (e.g., Rust et al., 1992), or preference as a evidence of viewing (e.g., Frank, Becknell, & Clokey, 1971) with little, if any, consideration. This theoretical sleight of hand has been the source of some confusion in the literature about audience behavior. In any event, program audiences are generally thought to form in strict adherence to the preferences of the available audience.

The second area of concern has to do with the structure of those preferences. Economists dealt with this as a theoretical abstraction by stating that there exist program types "defined in terms of viewer preferences" (Owen & Wildman, 1992, p. 72). *Program type* is a familiar concept. In television, we speak of soap operas, cop shows, and situation comedies. In radio, we describe station formats as middle-of-the-road, country, or all-news. To stipulate a viewer-defined typology forces us to consider exactly what categories of content are systematically related to audience likes and dislikes. In theory, such a typology must mean that people who like one type of program will like all other programs of that type. Conversely, people who dislike a type of program, must dislike all others of that type.

Marketing researchers approach this topic empirically by trying to identify those dimensions of content that are systematically related to viewer preferences. The hunt for viewer-defined program types began in the 1960s when analysts finally got the computing power they needed (e.g., Kirsch & Banks, 1962; Wells, 1969), and has proceeded intermittently since that time (e.g., Frank & Greenberg, 1980; Rao, 1975; Rust et al., 1992). Although there is reason to question the methods and theoretical assumptions of some studies (see Ehrenberg, 1968; Webster & Wakshlag, 1983), the findings suggest that common sense industry categories come as close to offering viewer-defined typology as anything else. That is to say, the people who like one soap opera do, in fact, tend to like other soap operas, and so on. Analogous work on music suggests a similar consistency of preference for various genres of music (Christenson & Peterson, 1988; Fink, Robinson, & Dowden, 1985).

This line of research supports the intuitively appealing conclusion that people's preferences for media offerings are systematically related to familiar categories of content. Two additional results from this line of research are worth noting. First, people's dislikes are more clearly related to program type than are their likes (Goodhardt, Ehrenberg, & Collins, 1987; Rust et al., 1992). In other words, what we like may be eclectic, but what we dislike is more readily categorized. Second, there is only a modest association between the structure of people's preferences and other individual or social traits. Frank et al. (1971) reported a slight correlation between network program preferences and conventional demographic groupings. More elaborate schemes of audience segmentation that relied on interests or needs produced similar results (e.g., Frank & Greenberg, 1980; Rust et al., 1992). In television, the absence of powerful correlations between content preference and demographics may be attributable to the "excessive sameness" of network programs. Still, it is worth noting that the research does not suggest any sort of rigid relationship between a person's preferences and his or her place in society.

Economists and market researchers are not alone in their theoretical commitment to program preference as the trait best able to explain audience behavior. *Selective exposure* offers a similar model for explaining people's use of media content. In its earliest form, selective exposure theory assumed that people had certain attitudes, beliefs, or convictions that they were disinclined to change. These predispositions led people to seek out communications that were consistent with their beliefs and avoid material that challenged them. Simply put, people were thought to see what they wanted to see, and hear what they wanted to hear.

This common sense notion gained greater credibility in the 1950s and 1960s with the introduction and testing of formal psychological theories like cognitive dissonance (Festinger, 1957). Early studies seemed to indicate that people did select media materials in such a way as to support their existing belief systems or cognitions. Hence, selective exposure to news and information appeared to be an important principle in understanding an individual's choice of media offerings.

By the 1970s, however, more exacting studies began to cast doubt on the lockstep nature of selective exposure to information (see Cotton, 1985; Sears & Freedman, 1967). Although research in this area languished for a time, more recent variations of the selective exposure hypothesis have been introduced. For example, experimental studies have shown that people's choices of entertainment vary with their moods and emotions (Wakshlag, Vial, & Tamborini, 1983; Zillmann & Bryant, 1985; Zillmann, Hezel, & Medoff, 1980). Excited or overstimulated people are more inclined to select relaxing program fare, whereas people who are bored are likely to choose stimulating content. Emotional states, in addition to more dispassionate cognitions, seem to influence our program preferences.

Gratificationist theory provides a closely related, if somewhat broader, perspective on audience behavior. Studies of uses and gratifications, as they are often called, are the work of social psychologists. This approach emerged in the early 1970s, partly as a reaction against the field's apparent obsession with media effects research. Gratificationists argued that we should ask not only "what media do to people," but also "what people do with the media." The research agenda of this approach was spelled out by Katz, Blumler, and Gurevitch (1974). According to them, gratificationists

are concerned with (1) the social and psychological origins of (2) needs, which generate (3) expectations of (4) mass media or other sources, which lead to (5) differential patterns of media exposure (or engagement in other activities), resulting in (6) need gratifications and (7) other consequences, perhaps mostly unintended ones. (p. 20)

Since the early 1970s, gratificationist research and theory has attracted considerable attention (see Rosengren, Wenner, & Palmgreen, 1985). Of greatest relevance to our discussion is the gratificationist's approach to explaining patterns of media exposure. Under this perspective, those patterns are determined by each person's expectations of how well different media or program content will gratify their needs. Such needs might be short-lived, like those associated with mood states, or relatively constant. In any event, it seems likely that the gratifications being sought translate rather directly into preferences for the media and their content.

Gratificationist theory, therefore, has much in common with economic models of program choice and theories of selective exposure. All of these cast individual preferences, however they have emerged, as the central mechanism for explaining exposure. Once these psychological predispositions are in place, they seem to translate in a direct, unproblematic way to program choices. Under this theoretical framework, understanding audience behavior is basically a matter of ascertaining content preferences and aggregating the result.

Unfortunately, the power of preferences to determine exposure to the media is not as absolute as many have assumed. There are a number of audience studies that attest to this breakdown.

In 1963, Gary Steiner published a landmark audience survey, *The People Look at Television*. That study, and subsequent replications (Bower, 1973, 1985) drew the linkage between preference and exposure into serious question:

> Another, seemingly peculiar, finding of Steiner in 1960 was the lack of relationship between expressed attitudes toward television and the public's actual patterns of viewing. . . . It seemed peculiar because social scientists often seek and usually find a congruence between attitudes and behavior. Steiner's finding might have been set aside as another of those one-time flukes that appear in social research had we not had the opportunity to examine it twice more—in 1970 by replicating the 1960 procedures in Minneapolis/St. Paul and in 1980 by a "last-night's" viewing diary. It would not be accurate to say that in the two replications *no* relationship was found between what people said and what they did, but certainly it was a minuscule one. (Bower, 1985, p. 132)

Another large-scale study, featuring elaborate schemes of audience segmentation based on needs, interests, and conventional demographics, produced a similar result:

> The interest segmentation scheme accounts for differences in program type television viewing behavior as well as the demographic scheme does . . . neither segmentation scheme separately nor both of them in combination,

however, explain a very high percentage in the variation in viewing behavior. (Frank & Greenberg, 1980, p. 218)

Nor do the patterns of program-type loyalty found in preference data seem to manifest themselves in analogous patterns of viewing. Based on a long-standing program of audience research dating back to the 1960s marketing researchers concluded, "there is no special tendency across the population for people who watch one programme of a given type to also watch others of the same type" (Goodhardt et al., 1987, p. 45).

These results do not mean that audience preferences are irrelevant to audience behavior, but they do imply that these factors are not as closely linked as is widely assumed. There are several explanations for the disparity between what people say or think and what they actually do. In the electronic media, the most obvious explanation are the patterns of audience availability reviewed earlier. Although many theorists tend to ignore this factor, outside the laboratory it effectively constrains program choice. Because availability is generally unrelated to content, it infuses audience behavior with an apparent randomness. Another part of the explanation can be found in the way media offerings are structured. These factors are examined in detail in the pages to come. Still another part of the explanation can be found in the remaining microlevel audience factors.

Most research and theory on the relationship between preference and choice focuses on the individual, and assumes that personal preferences can be freely exercised in the selection of media content. Much of our media use, however, is done not in isolation, but in the company of others. This is especially true of television viewing and moviegoing. Even with the advent of multitelevision households and video cassette recorders (VCRs), *group viewing* is a common phenomenon (Bower, 1985).

What little research there is about the dynamics of group viewing suggests that negotiation among competing preferences is quite usual (Bogart, 1972; Lull, 1982; Morley, 1986). Different members of the family seem to exercise more or less influence at different times of the day. For example, programmers make much of the fact that children are often in control of the television set in the late afternoon when they return from school (Eastman, 1993). Exposure to television programming, then, results not only from who is available and what they like, but who is actually making the program selections. People get their first choices some of the time, but can be outvoted at other times. If they are overruled, however, they will often stay with the viewing group. Like availability, this has the effect of making program choices seem more random with respect to content. That randomness is most pronounced when the composition of the decision-making group varies over time (Webster & Wakshlag, 1982).

The last audience factor to enter the picture is *awareness*. By awareness, we mean a knowledge of the media offerings that are available to you. Much theorizing about the audience presupposes a perfect awareness on the part of audience members. In other words, program selection is assumed to occur with a full knowledge of programming options. Although that assumption might be workable on a very abstract level, or in very simple media environments, it does not seem to work well in the media-rich environments that confront most audience members (Heeter, 1988; Heeter & Greenberg, 1985).

If, as is sometimes the case, people select media offerings without a full understanding of their options, the interpretation of choice as an expression of preference is complicated. How many times have you missed an interesting magazine article because you did not know it was there? How often have you discovered a favorite program or song long after it first aired? As more and more media compete for the attention of the audience, these sorts of breakdowns between preference and choice are likely to be increasingly common.

The role that audience preferences play in determining audience behavior, then, is far less tidy than we might wish. If an item of content attracts a small audience, it might indicate that people found it unappealing. But it could also be that the desired audience was unavailable, or perhaps people just did not know the content was there for the taking. Furthermore, audience factors are only half of the picture. The structure of the media themselves have a powerful impact on patterns of exposure.

MEDIA FACTORS

As with audience factors, media factors can be categorized as structural or individual. The structural attributes of the media complement the structural features of the mass audience. They include market conditions, modes of distribution, and the organization of available content. Individual level media factors vary in tandem with individual audience attributes, defining differences in the media environment from household to household.

Structural Features of the Media

The first structural characteristic of the media that should be taken into account is *coverage*. This is the extent to which people are physically able to receive a particular media offering. Newspapers tend to circulate in geographically defined market areas. Although some publications are readily available to a national readership, most are unseen and therefore unread. Films and other forms of print media depend on the idiosyncrasies of their own distribution systems to reach prospective audiences (Bagdikian, 1992; Gomery, 1993; Vogel, 1994). In theory, postal services, libraries, and computer networks can help mitigate variable coverage by offering media on demand. But as a practical matter, now, and in the foreseeable future, what the media serve up is an important determinant of what the audience consumes.

Even the most pervasive of all media, radio and television, are surprisingly spotty in the coverage they afford. In the United States, the universal availability of broadcasting is usually taken for granted. In other countries, especially in developing nations, universal coverage is not the rule. Even in the United States, newer forms of media are not available to all households. Table 2.2 summarizes the growth of various electronic media in this country.

Obviously, a medium's coverage of the population has a powerful impact on its ability to attract audiences. Early television audiences had to be small because few people had receivers. Similarly, cable television's audiences are shaped, in the first instance, by the fact that less than two thirds of U.S. households subscribe to that medium. Indeed, barring some major change in the technology and/or regulation of newer media, it is unlikely that any will achieve the coverage of major broadcast networks.

Even traditional networks, however, have certain vagaries in their coverage. With the exception of a few stations that are actually owned and operated ("O & Os") by the networks, affiliates are independent businesses that act in their own self-interest. This means that an affiliate may not carry all of a network's programming if it believes some other offering will be more profitable. A commitment on the part of a station to hold its schedule open for a network-fed program is called *network clearance*. Usually, of course, an affiliate will clear its network's programming. Sometimes, however, a network program, particularly one that is unpopular, will not get clearance on all affiliates (Besen, Krattenmaker, Metzger, & Woodbury, 1984; Owen & Wildman, 1992). If this happens on enough affiliates, or even a few affiliates in larger markets, it can seriously erode the network's coverage, compounding the problem of a low-rated show.

All these aspects of program or network coverage impose real physical limits on what programming is available to particular audiences. For that reason, they are powerful determinants of audience size. But the structural attributes of the media go beyond channel or program availability. On each channel, there is a certain sequence of programming that affects patterns of exposure. Although the ability to tape and replay programming can, in principle, break this rigid structure, in practice, relatively little taping is done. Program scheduling, in and across channels, therefore, is widely believed to be an important factor in shaping the size, composition, and flow of audiences.

TABLE 2.2
Growth of Electronic Media in the United States

Year	Total U.S. Households	Percentage of Households With						
		Radio	TV	Cable	Pay Cable	VCRs	Computers	Computers Online
1930	30,000,000	46%						
1940	35,000,000	81%						
1950	43,000,000	95%	9%					
1960	53,000,000	96%	87%					
1970	61,000,000	98%	95%	6%				
1980	78,000,000	98%	98%	19%	6%	1%		
1990	94,000,000	99%	98%	55%	28%	67%	23%	1.6%
1991	94,000,000	99%	98%	58%	29%	71%	25%	2.0%
1992	94,000,000	99%	98%	59%	28%	73%	28%	2.6%
1993	95,000,000	99%	98%	60%	27%	76%	30%	3.3%
1994	96,000,000	99%	98%	61%	27%	77%	32%	4.7%
1995	97,000,000	99%	98%	62%	28%	80%	35%	7.5%

Sources: Lichty & Topping (1975); Veronis, Suhler, & Associates (1995); Webster & Lichty (1991)

The first factor to consider is the number of program options that confront the audience. For almost all media, the sheer number of choices before the audience has increased. This is especially true for television; the average American household now receives some 40 different channels of programming (Nielsen Media Research, 1993).

Virtually all of these channels are competing for the audience, although they may employ different strategies in doing so. The economic theories reviewed earlier in the chapter provide a model for understanding how competitors will behave in their pursuit of the mass audience. Indeed, an important purpose of those theories is illuminating how audiences and media structure interact. Essentially, if it is assumed that there is a relatively large audience for some particular type of programming, then two or more channels or stations will split that audience by offering programming of that type. In theory, this will continue to happen until that program type audience has been divided into small enough pieces that it makes sense for the next competitor to offer a different kind of programming (Owen & Wildman, 1992). In practice, this strategy is called *counterprogramming* (Eastman, 1993; Lin, 1995; Tiedge & Ksobiech, 1987).

When there are only a few competitors, the models suggest there will be an excessive sameness about program offerings. Each channel tries to maximize its audience with "lowest common denominator" programming. However, as the number of competitors increases, program services are expected to become more differentiated (Waterman, 1992). This process continues until potential audiences are so small as to make it unlikely that one will recover the costs of providing a program service. We develop this line of reasoning in greater detail in chapter 7.

Presenting the audience with an array of competing services has two important consequences. First, from the individual's point of view, programs are offered up as a series of forced choices. It is quite possible to encounter situations in which two desirable programs are appearing on television at the same time. After all, presenting the viewer with tough choices is what the competition is all about. Had those shows been scheduled at different times, the viewer could have watched both. But, given the nature of the program schedule, a choice is forced. This kind of competitive scheduling is another reason why a person's preferences may not be the best guide to actual patterns of exposure. Second, when individual choices are aggregated, an increased number of competitors will fragment the audience.

Audience fragmentation is a matter of breaking the mass audience into smaller and smaller segments. It seems to be an inevitable outcome of allowing greater competition for the audience, at least if competitors are more or less equally matched. In most large radio markets, for example, one station cannot expect to consistently dominate the others. Each targets a segment of the audience and must usually settle for a share of audience in the single digits. The same is true in television, although as our discussion on coverage indicates, some of the competitors have a considerable advantage. We explore the implications of this new media environment in chapter 7.

The structural attributes of media are also associated with well-established features of audience duplication. *Audience duplication* is the extent to which two different programs have an audience in common. When those programs are scheduled in adjacent time periods, duplication is usually referred to as audience flow. Patterns of audience flow can certainly affect the size of any one program's audience, but the study of audience duplication involves cumulative measurements.

The best-known pattern of audience flow is called an *inheritance effect*, which occurs between programs that are scheduled back-to-back on the same channel (Goodhardt et al., 1987; Walker, 1988; Webster, 1985). When one program ends, an unusually large percentage of its audience will stay tuned to the following program. That is, there is an especially high level of audience duplication between adjacent shows on the same channel. Obviously, if the first, or *lead-in* program has a large audience, the following program stands to benefit. This feature of audience flow has given rise to a number of television programming strategies including *hammocking, tent-poling,* and *block programming* (Eastman, 1993). The various factors that determine inheritance effects are discussed in chapter 4.

A second pattern of audience duplication is called *repeat viewing*. It is the level of audience duplication between different episodes in a series. For programs that are stripped five times a week, the episodes are only a day apart. For other series, like those in prime time, they are a week apart. Most research about repeat viewing has used diary data, and has therefore concentrated on stripped programming. These studies indicate that the typical level of repeat viewing is in the order of 50% (Goodhardt et al., 1987) More recent studies using peoplemeter data find more variable, yet highly predictable, repeat viewing rates (Webster & Wang, 1992). The determinants of repeat viewing are dealt with at length in chapter 5.

A third feature of audience duplication is *channel loyalty*. Like inheritance effects, this is a predictable kind of audience duplication between different programs on the same channel. In this case however, the programs can be scheduled days apart. The level of audience duplication is not as great as that found with adjacent programs, but is still greater than chance. Many researchers have found evidence of channel loyalty, but the most extensive program of research was conducted by Goodhardt et al. (1987). According to their reports, people who watch a channel one day are more likely than the general public to watch it again on another day. The level of audience loyalty varies somewhat from channel to channel. But for the major U.S. networks, it appears that the audience for one network show is 50% to 60% more likely than the population in general to watch that network on another day. This method of analysis has been codified in what Goodhardt et al. (1987) called the *duplication of viewing law*. The law is discussed in greater length in chapter 4.

Why channel loyalty exists is something of a mystery. Its relationship to program content is problematic at best (Brosius, Wober, & Weimann, 1992; Goodhardt et al., 1987). It seems more easily explained, at least in part, by underlying patterns of audience availability. For example, channel loyalty is higher in the late afternoon and late at night. During these time periods, large blocks of the audience are consistently unavailable, thus the remaining audience is, by default, more likely to show up in program audiences on a day-to-day basis. Similarly, when we look for channel loyalty among viewers who all watch the same amount of television (i.e., have similar amounts of available time), the phenomenon seems to disappear.

We have seen how structural aspects of the media themselves interact with audience factors to produce major patterns of media exposure. Although our review has concentrated on electronic media, it is easy to imagine how the structural features of other media—the placement of stories in the newspaper, or the number of screens showing a film—shape mass exposure. Barring an unusual effort on the part of an audience member, these factors effectively constrain choices. In television, scheduling a number of programs opposite one another precludes exposure to all but one, even if they are equally appealing. Running a new program after an established hit increases the likelihood that it will be seen. Scheduling a new program after an unpopular show greatly reduces the probability of exposure. Programs scheduled on the same channel are more likely to have a duplicated audience than programs scheduled on different channels. Scheduling programs in adjacent time slots will increase audience duplication even further. There are, however, a few microlevel media factors that should be reviewed to complete the picture.

The Individual's Media Environment

Network coverage and program scheduling are generally beyond the control of an audience member. But certain aspects of the media environment are in the individual's control. In fact, this is more true today than it has ever been. As new technologies and programming alternatives enter the marketplace, each of us has greater latitude in shaping a media environment to suit our purposes. These decisions can certainly affect our exposure to the media and are closely related to the microlevel audience factors reviewed earlier.

Cable subscription is one such alternative for shaping a media environment. We touched on cable often in the preceding discussion. Although much about cable's organization and availability is appropriately conceptualized as a structural variable beyond a person's control, the decision to subscribe is ultimately made by each individual household. Cable, in other words, is not just something that is done to us, it is also something we elect to do. This self-selection into the cable universe is one reason why comparisons of cable and noncable households must be made with care.

The reason why people subscribe to cable varies from home to home (LaRose & Atkin, 1988). We do know that cable subscribers have higher incomes that nonsubscribers. We also know that cable households tend to have more people living in them. This is especially true of families that buy a pay-cable service (Ducey, Krugman, & Eckrich, 1983; Webster, 1983). With more children and more money to spend, subscription to cable probably makes sense. Gratificationists point out that users of new media may derive special psychological satisfactions from their viewing environment (Jacobs, 1995; Perse, 1990; Perse & Ferguson, 1993; Williams, Phillips, & Lum, 1985). Others undoubtedly subscribe just to improve the quality of over-the-air reception.

Researchers have also observed that cable subscribers have a somewhat different style of viewing television. Confronted with a large number of channels to choose from, cable subscribers apparently develop a *channel repertoire* (Heeter, 1988; Ferguson & Perse, 1993). This repertoire is a subset of total number of channels available to the subscriber. The more channels there are, the larger is the repertoire. But there is not a one-to-one correspondence. As the number of available channels increases, the proportion that are used decreases. The net result is that each cable viewer constructs an array of channels from which to choose on a day-to-day basis. This may effectively cancel out viewing on some channels, even if they can be received on the set.

VCRs are another microlevel factor that has received a considerable amount of scholarly attention (Dobrow, 1990; Levy, 1989; Lin, 1993). At the beginning of the 1980s, they were virtually nonexistent as a household appliance. Today, they have surpassed cable penetration and are in more than 80% of all households. Many analysts have likened their adoption curve to that of color television. If that is, indeed, a model of VCR growth, their penetration into U. S. households might ultimately exceed 90%.

VCR usage falls into two broad categories: time-shifting and library use. As the label suggests, time-shifting involves recording a program for replay at a more convenient time. Research indicates that the lag time between taping and replay varies with how often a program is broadcast (e.g., stripped shows are replayed faster than weekly offerings). It is also quite predictable: Levy and Fink (1984) likened the rate of replay to a radioactive decay curve. The most taped programs are those broadcast by the major networks. Many programs that are recorded for time-shifting are never played back.

The library uses of the VCR can involve off-the-air taping. But if that is done, it is with the intention of adding the tape to a "library." Increasingly, people will buy or rent tapes for viewing at home. In fact, virtually all VCR owners report that they use their machines to show rented cassettes. The most popular rentals are major motion pictures that were successful in theatrical release. As this market grows, however, more programming made specifically for home viewing is likely to be produced.

Despite these important changes, the total amount of time that people actually spend watching taped programming is tiny compared to the total amount of television that is consumed. For example, the time-shift audience for a prime-time network program rarely accounts for more than 1 rating point. That, of course, could change, and the impact of VCRs on patterns of exposure to electronic media should be carefully monitored.

The technology and deployment of receivers, is yet another aspect of the media environment over which people can exercise some control. Color television sets are now in 97% of all U.S. households. Nearly two thirds of homes now have more than one television set, and more than 20% have three or more sets. The location and capability of these receivers affect the quality of the media environment in the home (Pardun & Krugman, 1994).

One innovation in television set technology with implications for patterns of exposure to television is the *remote control* device (Eastman & Newton, 1995; Walker & Bellamy, 1993). Today, virtually all television households have a set with this feature, especially among main sets where most viewing occurs. Because they make channel changing so easy, remote control devices strike fear in the hearts of advertisers and programmers alike. From the advertiser's perspective, viewers may be more likely to change channels when an advertisement comes on. This practice, called *zapping*, could obviously reduce exposure to commercial messages. From the programmer's perspective, audiences lost during commercial breaks, or a lull in the program itself, may be difficult to regain. From the individual viewer's perspective, however, these are mundane behaviors of little consequence (Ferguson, 1994). Whether this phenomenon becomes a major factor in shaping the mass audience remains to be seen. The preliminary answer seems to be that the remote control device will not produce substantial behavioral changes (Eastman & Newton, 1995), but it bears watching.

A MODEL OF MASS AUDIENCE BEHAVIOR

Many things affect the behavior of the mass audience. We defined and discussed most of these factors in preceding sections of the chapter, but have not yet put the pieces of the puzzle together. It may be useful at this point to step back, reflect briefly on what has been presented, and then try to forge an overall framework for examining media exposure.

Audience researchers of all stripes have devoted time and effort to understanding people's use of the electronic media. Market researchers and programmers have engaged in very pragmatic studies of audience formation, economists have developed rather abstract theories of program choice, and social psychologists have performed a seemingly endless succession of experiments and surveys to reveal the origins of audience behavior. Despite real progress in these, and many other fields, there has been an unfortunate tendency for each group to work in isolation from the others. Instances of cross-pollination between theorists and practitioners, or even across different academic disciplines are all too rare.

At the risk of greatly oversimplifying matters, two fairly distinct approaches to understanding the audience can be identified. The first credits individuals with the power to determine exposure to the media, often to the exclusion of other factors. It tends to cast people in the role of active choice-makers, free to select whatever media suit their fancy. As such, this perspective is very much in keeping with intellectual trends in the field:

The notion of "the active communicator" is rapidly achieving preeminent status in the communication discipline. In the mass and interpersonal communication literatures alike, we read statement after statement claiming that today's message receivers have abundant message options and actively select from and act on these messages. (Bryant & Street, 1988, p. 162)

This perspective is typical of work in psychology, communication studies, and to some extent, marketing and economics. It also has enormous intuitive appeal, and is likely to characterize most "man-in-the-street" explanations of the audience. After all, audiences are simply collections of individuals. Surely, if we can understand behavior at the individual level, then our ability to explain larger patterns of mass behavior will follow. When we conceptualize audience behavior at the individual level, we tend to look for explanations by thinking of those things that distinguish us as individuals. Above all, we have invoked preferences (or needs and expectations) as a way to explain behavior. With this focus, however, we often miss seeing things that crystallize different levels of analysis. As William McPhee (1963) noted "most of our modern social research is irretrievably *microscopic*; that is it is only about individuals in the mass" (p. 4).

The second perspective is more inclined to conceive of the mass audience as a dynamic entity in its own right and emphasize structural factors as principle determinants of mass behavior. It does not necessarily assume that people are passive, but it is cognizant of the fact that the actions of audience members are shaped by outside forces like work schedules and the structure of media offerings. It is only within these constraints that "activity," in the usual sense, is likely to operate. As such, the concept of activity is less central to this theoretical perspective.

This approach is more typical of work in sociology, human ecology, media planning, and welfare economics. It downplays individual needs and wants, and concentrates on things like total audience size, the structure of media distribution systems, and program schedules in attempting to understand audience behavior. Although work in this area can be highly successful at creating statistical explanations of aggregated data, it occasionally has a hollow ring to it. One is often tempted to ask what this means in human terms—what does it tell us about ourselves? Such explanations are sometimes possible, but not always apparent.

It is important to recognize that neither approach is right or wrong. It is also important to note that neither approach is fully complete without the other. Despite the fact that these models of audience behavior are sometimes advanced as mutually exclusive alternatives, we believe that there is much to be gained by trying to integrate them. Specifically, analyses of individual behavior might be enhanced by a more deliberate consideration of the structural factors suggested here. We know, through observation, that these variables are highly correlated with audience behavior, and weaving them into microlevel studies might increase the latter's power and generalizability. Conversely, research in mass behavior might be more explicit about its relationship to theoretical concepts that are central in the individual approach. This could improve its popular acceptance and utility. It is in this spirit that we propose the following model.

We used the term model rather loosely throughout this chapter. In fact, it has several meanings. In its broadest sense, it can mean an entire way of looking at the world, as implied by the term scientific model. Conceiving of the audience as a mass might be thought of as a model in that sense. A model can also imply an exacting level of precision. A mathematical or computer model requires that relationships among the elements of the model be quantified. The literature on mass audience behavior is rife with such models (e.g., Barnett et al., 1991; Goodhardt et al., 1987; Henriksen, 1985; Rust, 1986). A model can also mean a guide or heuristic device, useful in thinking through phenomena of interest.

The model presented in Fig. 2.2 is a model in the latter sense of the word. It is intended to help organize and stimulate our thinking about audience behavior. It suggests a few broad relationships, but it does not, in and of itself, provide hypotheses to be tested. It certainly falls short of being a mathematical model, although it is useful in situating the empirical models presented in the chapters that follow.

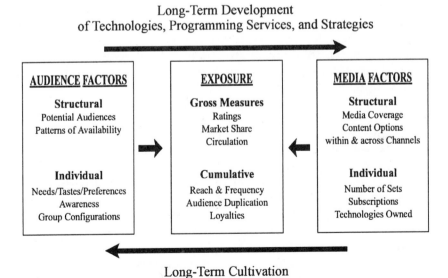

Long-Term Development
of Technologies, Programming Services, and Strategies

AUDIENCE FACTORS	EXPOSURE	MEDIA FACTORS
Structural	**Gross Measures**	**Structural**
Potential Audiences	Ratings	Media Coverage
Patterns of Availability	Market Share	Content Options
	Circulation	within & across Channels
Individual	**Cumulative**	**Individual**
Needs/Tastes/Preferences	Reach & Frequency	Number of Sets
Awareness	Audience Duplication	Subscriptions
Group Configurations	Loyalties	Technologies Owned

Long-Term Cultivation
of Tastes, Expectations, and Habits

FIG. 2.2. A model of mass audience behavior. Adapted from Webster and Lichty, 1991.

The central component of the model, the thing we are trying to explain, is exposure to media. As we argued in the beginning of the chapter, exposure is the defining characteristic of the mass audience. The behavior of the mass is most often expressed as gross measures of audience size and composition or cumulative measures like reach and frequency. Two types of factors determine exposure: audience factors and media factors. The direction of influence is indicated by arrows. For example, the model stipulates that audience factors cause ratings, not the reverse. There are also cause and effect relationships among the factors in each box. For instance, audience needs probably contribute to patterns of availability, and cable subscription helps shape cable network coverage. We opted to omit arrows suggesting these interrelationships to keep the model a bit cleaner.

To understand mass audience behavior, we advocate considering structural explanations first. There are three reasons why we recommend this approach. First, like the mass behavior we are trying to explain, they are pitched at a macrolevel of analysis. Because structural factors tend to be a uniform presence across large numbers of people, their effect is often easier to detect. Second, structural factors are more knowable. Information on program schedules, network coverage, and total audiences is routinely reported. Individual factors, like audience awareness and the use of remote control devices, are harder to pin down. Third, we know from experience that structural explanations work. Statistically speaking, it is not unusual to find three or four structural factors explaining a large portion of the variance in mass audience behavior. Indeed, structures are so important for explaining patterns of exposure in the field, we argue they have become an essential element of mass audience thinking. If structures fail to provide a satisfying answer, however, the next step would be the process of thinking through the individual-level factors on either side of the model.

It is important to note the limitations of this exercise in modeling. As the preceding pages of this book indicate, there are many ways of conceiving of an audience and many things about audiencehood we might wish to know. This model tells us very little about what the media mean to people or the role they play in our lives. These are significant questions that have attracted considerable attention in the academy, and they will undoubtedly continue to do so. Instead, we focus on important, but very particularized, questions of audience. How do large numbers of people come into contact with the real world of media? What determines exposure? What explains the behavior of the mass?

Even with that qualification, a further caution is in order. The model focuses primarily on short-term features of audience behavior. It defines exposure as the result, but not the cause, of other factors. It assumes, as does much of the research we reviewed, that individual preferences exist a priori, independent of market forces and the culture at large. In the short-term, this is a workable assumption, but over the long haul, it is problematic. In fact, it has been a major criticism of economic models of program choice (Gandy, 1992).

Certainly, many of the most interesting questions about the mass audience are long-term in nature. Over a period of months, or even weeks, ratings can have a substantial effect on the structure of the media. Programs are canceled, new shows developed, schedules altered, and clearances changed, often on the basis of audience behavior. In fact, this is the genesis of the audience power we described in chapter 1.

To keep these issues in mind, we have specified some long-term relationships between audience and media factors. For example, the growth of potential audiences and patterns of availability clearly affect the development of media services and programming strategies. Conversely, the structure and content of the media undoubtedly cultivate certain tastes, expectations, and habits on the part of the audience. These are important relationships that merit further investigation. Bearing such limitations in mind, we hope the model can, nonetheless, provide a useful framework for understanding mass audience behavior and the empirical studies that follow.

Chapter 3

The Audience Commodity

One of the principal reasons for conceiving of the audience as a mass is to facilitate economic exchange. Since the earliest days of mass media, readers and, in their turn, listeners and viewers have been counted up and sold to advertisers—a practice that has effectively turned the audience into a commodity. Viewed in this light, media content is simply the bait that is offered to lure people into an audience. Economists and other social scientists have come to recognize that the real product of the media is the audience—a conclusion that most practitioners would find self-evident. The words of a media sales executive serve as an apt representation of this perspective:

> I can't think of any other business that makes one product but sells another product. If you think about it, we make programs and put them on the air. We are not selling the programs, we are selling the people that watch the programs. . . so there is no direct correlation between that audience and that product that we are putting on the air. (Phalen, 1996, p. 76).

Obviously, the people who buy and sell advertising are acutely aware of the need to attract, measure, and assign economic value to the audience. But they generally do this without much theorizing about their own practices or the social consequences of the enterprise. For media professionals, the audience commodity is simply an economic fact of life. Our purpose in this chapter is to analyze the trade in audiences from the perspective of how economic value is determined. The study that we present here illustrates a practical and important application of mass audience thinking in economic exchange.

There are several theoretical perspectives that can be brought to bear on the consideration of audience as commodity. Although the practice of selling advertising space based on audience numbers was well-established by the late 19th century, critical scholars have only recently begun to contemplate the commodification of audiences. In a seminal work on the subject, Smythe (1977) accused Western Marxism of having a blindspot in failing to consider the real commodity produced by the "consciousness industry"—the audience. This was followed by a number of research efforts including analyses of how the audience produces value, whether audience members are adequately compensated for their labor (Jhally & Livant, 1986; Maxwell, 1991; Smythe, 1981), and how the ratings industry contributes to the market for audiences (Ang, 1991; Hurwitz, 1983; Meehan, 1984). In a related line of work, critics broadened the scope of their concerns to consider how the use of personal information affords institutions a measure of control over the public (e.g., Gandy, 1993; Larson, 1992).

The audience commodity has also been the subject of more traditional forms of economic analysis. This perspective, which is generally taken by neoclassical economists in studies of the television marketplace (Besen 1976; Fisher, McGowan, & Evans, 1980; Owen & Wildman, 1992), recognizes that media are in the business of creating and selling the audience. As media economist Bruce Owen and his coauthors bluntly pointed out:

> The first and most serious mistake that an analyst of the television industry can make is to assume that TV stations are in business to produce programs. They are not. TV stations are in the business of producing audiences. These audiences, or means of access to them, are sold to advertisers. The product of a TV station is measured in dimensions of people and time. The price of the product is quoted in dollars per thousand viewers per minute of commercial time. (Owen, Beebe, & Manning, 1974, p. 4)

There is broad recognition, then, that the true product of advertiser-supported media is the audience. Beyond that insight, however, approaches to the study of the audience diverge rather sharply. The approach we adopt in this chapter is more closely allied with a mainstream neoclassical perspective on the subject. We focus our attention on the trade in audiences and how market forces help determine the prices that are paid for that commodity. Methodologically, we employ a fairly traditional brand of empiricism—quantifying independent and dependent variables to statistically assess their relationships. Although many theoretical premises of our analysis could be as easily applied to print as to broadcasting, as we have done elsewhere in this book, we focus our attention on television.

THE TRADE IN AUDIENCES

In the United States alone, some $35 billion is spent for television commercial time each year (Television Bureau of Advertising, 1995). The market includes thousands of advertisers who buy time in the hopes of reaching an audience of potential customers. These organizations range from large consumer goods corporations that buy millions of dollars in airtime each season to smaller "mom and pop" companies that buy only a few hundred dollars worth of inventory annually. Subject to budget constraints and marketing plans, they have several options for reaching the television audience: broadcast networks, cable networks, syndication, national spot, unwired networks, local market stations, and local cable systems. Each media option attracts a slightly different audience and features different selling points.

The immediate goal of the time buyer is to find the right audience for the best price. The desired consumers are often described by a handful of demographic traits (e.g., age, gender, etc.), although complex schemes of audience segmentation have become increasingly popular (Larson, 1992). The purchase of an audience can be a straightforward transaction between buyer and seller but, in the modern media marketplace, it is usually more complicated. Figure 3.1 is a schematic diagram of the market for television

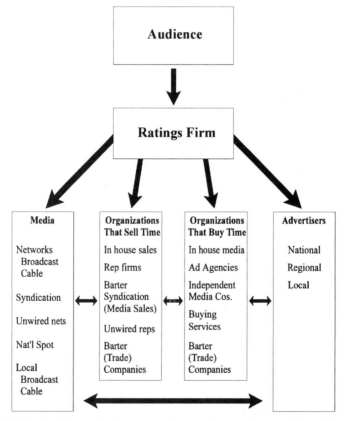

FIG. 3.1. Participants in the market for television audiences. Adapted from Phalen, 1996.

audiences. It is an extension of the industry description provided by Owen and Wildman (1992). As the reader will note, several types of firms intervene in the process of buying and selling commercial time. Although we generally speak of the economic exchange as taking place between media and advertisers, the actual transactions often occur between independent companies that represent each side in negotiations. Depending on the geographic location of the desired audience (national, regional, or local), agencies will conduct negotiations on behalf of advertisers, and rep firms or sales organizations will negotiate on behalf of the media.

The *national spot market*, which is the focus of the quantitative analysis reported in this chapter, illustrates the complexity of trading relationships. The audience reached through national spot advertising consists of viewers who are located in some combination of local television markets. The upper half of the figure indicates that the audience is typically known to market participants through data collected and distributed by a ratings firm. This is a feature of the industry that we discuss in more detail later. Reading across the lower half of the chart in Fig. 3.1, the key players in the national spot market are local broadcast stations, rep firms, media buyers, and national or regional advertisers. The station generally has its own sales force to handle local businesses that buy only the local market, and it relies on salespeople at its national rep firm to make time available to nonlocal advertisers. Ordinarily, national spot is used to reach a targeted geographical area, although it is possible to build a national audience this way as well. Rep firms handle the logistics of selling the time, getting the commercials on the air, and making sure that the station gets paid. They do this for a commission on time sales.

Although each of the different media options claims its own business practices, there are some common elements involved in media sales. In the case where a decision to advertise on television has already been made, advertisers or their representatives contact media salespeople to discuss commercial availability and cost. Before that call is placed, a great deal of time and energy is spent analyzing audience information in order to plan the best commercial schedule for the advertiser. This planning is typically done by the media department at an agency. Negotiations follow in which each side bargains on the expected audience for a program or daypart, and on the fair market price to reach that audience (see Phalen, 1996; Poltrack, 1983).

Everyone involved in the business of buying and selling airtime is aware that attracting certain audiences is key to increasing the value of advertising time. In fact, consideration of the audience becomes second nature to market participants who speak of creating new audiences, of stealing audiences from competitors, and of losing or building audiences throughout the run of a program. They distinguish between programs that will appeal to the mass audience and those that will have a more narrow, targeted appeal, but they do not need or want to know everything about viewers. It is enough to understand who comes into contact with media, along with whatever characteristics make the audience attractive to advertisers. This is very much in keeping with what we described elsewhere as mass audience thinking.

All of this means that knowledge of the audience is a critical component of any marketplace exchange, and it suggests that a key element in the continued support of media by commercial concerns is the capacity to measure viewership. Without this measurement capability, the audience would remain unknown and, in a practical sense, unknowable to market participants. To address this need, the broadcast industry has developed a system for measuring and reporting audiences that facilitates the buying and selling of advertising time—the system of audience ratings (Beville, 1988; Webster & Lichty, 1991). The effect of the ratings is to make the invisible audience visible to market participants in some economically useful way.

As shown in Fig. 3.1, ratings information is collected and sold to all market participants. That information becomes the common knowledge that is circulated in the marketplace, and it provides buyers and sellers with a mutually acceptable point of reference in their discussions about the audience. At the present time, television ratings in the United States are the exclusive domain of the A.C. Nielsen Company, which reports on national as well as local television audiences. Nielsen maintains one national sample, which is measured with *peoplemeters*, and more than 200 local market samples that are measured by a combination of meters to capture set tuning behavior, and diaries to supply specific information on viewer characteristics. Estimates for national audiences and for audiences in metered markets are generated daily. Ratings in diary markets are generated several times each year. This information is used in media planning to predict audiences for upcoming programs, and in *post-buy analyses* to evaluate programming that has already aired.

Audience ratings data are of enormous importance to the television industry. As Larson (1992) noted:

> Most viewers know Nielsen only as the maker of the bullets that killed such shows as "Star Trek" and "Twin Peaks," but to think of its ratings exclusively in terms of their show-stopping power is to underestimate the depth of Nielsen's influence over the culture, content, and business of television and, therefore, over the evolution of our consumer culture itself. Nielsen *is* television. Imagine a company like IBM ceding to an outside party decisive control over whether it has a profit or loss in a given quarter, and you'll get a glimpse of Nielsen's peculiar hold over broadcasting. (pp. 105–106)

To many, this "peculiar hold" is synonymous with absolute power. However, the ratings industry is not as all-powerful as some would suggest, despite the tremendous influence that audience measurement has on the operation of commercial mass media. Although the people who buy and sell audiences on a daily basis may, out of necessity, treat audience numbers as "gospel," most users are more sophisticated. They recognize that audience ratings are estimates subject to sampling error and the messy world of data collection (Phalen, 1996). From time to time, the consumers of these data, aspiring competitors, or congressional investigators challenge the way that Nielsen does business. Even critics of the system acknowledge its capacity for self-correction:

> Plainly the Nielsen system has had its shortcomings, but in the end there are strong pressures to keep it honest. For one thing, advertisers want to get their money's worth, and therefore want a count that is at least internally consistent. If it is in the interest of the networks to overcount audiences—or at least the wealthiest eighteen-to-forty-nine-year-old segment that spends the most money—it is assuredly not in their interest to lose credibility with advertisers who pay the networks' way. (Gitlin, 1983, p. 53)

Even if everyone treated audience ratings as sacrosanct, a number of other factors would limit the power of these data to determine the price of the audience. For one thing, we should note that a trade in audiences can occur without the benefit of ratings. This happens in many radio markets, as well as in local television markets where Nielsen does not provide cable audience estimates. Absent ratings data, cable salespeople must convince potential clients that viewers are watching, even though they have no proof of that viewership. To do so, they pitch what they have. This includes citing national estimates that may suggest the character of the local audience, prestige factors (to be associated with ESPN, for example), or selling a geographically targeted reach that corresponds to retail trade areas. Although ratings data would presumably facilitate this exchange (Barnes & Thomson, 1994), the pursuit of the audience occurs nonetheless.

A more fundamental curb on the power of ratings data is revealed through a closer consideration of what is actually being purchased. The commodity audience that is bought and sold in the market is really a *probable audience* rather than an actual audience. Although it is true that the industry measures the audience and packages this information in a way that facilitates the buying and selling of advertising time, it is not the actual viewers that are being sold, but a probability of reaching those viewers—a probability that is conveniently expressed as a rating. All transactions that are conducted today are based on an estimate of tomorrow's audiences, and ratings form the basis of those estimates. As Webster and Lichty (1991) observed:

> It is important to remember that all ratings data are historical. They describe something that has already happened. It is equally important to remember that the buying and selling of audiences is always conducted in anticipation of future events. Although it is certainly useful to know which program had the largest audience last week, what really determines the allocation of advertising dollars is an expectation of who will have the largest audience next week or next season. (p. 208)

Ratings data cannot, in and of themselves, foretell the future. They are only a tool that human beings use to come to some agreement about what is likely to happen. As a consequence, the accuracy with which future audiences can be predicted from past ratings is an important consideration in the market for advertising time. If there is too much statistical error in ratings estimates, or if the media environment has changed substantially since the ratings were collected, the data become less useful in allocating advertising dollars.

Uncertainty in the data is addressed in several ways. After an advertising message runs, a post-buy analysis looks at how closely the purchased audience matches the actual audience. If the projections agreed on are much smaller than the actual ratings, then the advertiser can negotiate for additional time to make up for the audience deficiency. It is not always possible for the media to give these *make good* spots, either because there is too little inventory available or because the time that is available is not acceptable to the buyer. In those cases, other arrangements, such as giving cash back to the advertiser, might be implemented. There is no uniform policy about this, and each deal is different. But the commercial time is not paid for until both advertiser and broadcaster are happy with the way that the schedule has run. This effectively gives advertisers some certainty that the estimated audiences will be delivered.

The popular notion that ratings data, however flawed, completely determine the price of the audience commodity, is too simplistic. It is a much more complicated and human process than this single variable model suggests. Like any other exchange of goods and services, a host of market forces may affect the selling price. Moreover, the trade in audiences occurs between institutions that are staffed by real people with their own biases and professional networks (Phalen, 1996). These biases affect the price-setting process. Additionally, buyers and sellers often engage in a certain amount of gamesmanship in negotiations, seeking to exercise whatever advantages they may have. Although audiences, real or imagined, are certainly the principal determinant of the prices that are paid, the exchange is tempered by many other factors. We consider at least some of these in the following section.

DETERMINANTS OF ECONOMIC VALUE

The price that advertisers are willing to pay for commercial time is largely related to the audience that is expected for a program or time period. This audience may be created at one moment in time, as is the case with broadcast network programs, or it may accumulate over a week or more, as happens with barter syndicated programs. Unsurprisingly, any number of studies have verified that the size and composition of the television audience are major determinants of what prospective buyers will pay (e.g., Fournier & Martin, 1983; Fratrik, 1989; Wirth & Bloch, 1985). But even when one controls for such obvious sources of variation, many differences in the price of the audience remain unexplained. Across local television markets, for example, there are considerable differences in the going rate for a thousand viewers (Poltrack, 1983). These market-to-market discrepancies present an opportunity to examine how various structural features of the media marketplace could affect the selling price of local audiences. In fact, a limited number of studies have done just that. These studies are summarized in Table 3.1, and a few of the more influential are discussed here.

Besen (1976) was among the first to study the role of structural variables in establishing the value of television time. Although his unit of analysis was the station rather than the market, he found a number of interesting relationships that can be extended to an analysis of the television market as a whole. The dependent variable in his study was the rate that a station charged for a unit of advertising time. Although he found that the size of the potential audience had a positive effect on the station rate, he also determined that competitive characteristics of the station and the market exercised some influence. Specifically, stations in larger markets with few competitors were able to charge more for their broadcast time.

Fisher, McGowan, and Evans (1980), who studied the effects of cable television penetration on broadcast station revenue, found that audience size and characteristics, station type, and time of day were important predictors. They also considered median household income as a measure of market affluence, and found a positive relationship between that variable and revenue. They interpreted this as meaning that "richer populations are worth more to advertisers and hence to stations" (p. 700).

Poltrack (1983) studied the effects of economic and structural variables on television station income across markets. He identified substantial pricing differences among markets and discussed several factors that could contribute to this variability. These factors included general economic conditions, the number of viable local independent stations, and the com-

TABLE 3.1
Determinants of Economic Value[*]

Potential Determinants	References[1]
Size of Audience or Market	Besen (1976)
	Fisher et al. (1980)
	Fournier & Martin (1983)
	Fratrik (1989)
	Levin (1980)
	Takada & Henry (1993)
	Wirth & Bloch (1985)
Audience Demographic Composition	Fisher et al. (1980)
	Fournier & Martin (1983)
	Fratrik (1989)
Audience Location (ADI/TSA)	Fisher et al. (1980)
	Fratrik (1989)
	Poltrack (1983)
Certainty of Audience Delivery	Fournier & Martin (1983)
Daypart	Fisher et al. (1980)
	Poltrack (1983)
Overall Strength of Market Economy	Poltrack (1983)
	Vogel (1994)
Number of Stations in the Market	Besen (1976)
	Fournier & Martin (1983)
	Fratrik (1989)
	Levin (1980)
	Poltrack (1983)
Number & Circulation of Newspapers	Poltrack (1983)
Market Power or Concentration	Fournier & Martin (1983)
	Wirth & Bloch (1985)
Ratio of National Spot to Local Revenue	Poltrack (1983)
Level of Cable Penetration	Fratrik (1989)
	Wirth & Bloch (1985)
VHF versus UHF	Besen (1976)
	Fisher et al. (1980)
	Fratrik (1989)
	Levin (1980)
Network Affiliation or Ownership	Besen (1976)
	Fisher et al. (1980)
	Fournier & Martin (1983)
	Takada & Henry (1993)
Total Levels of Media Use in Market	Poltrack (1983)
Season of the Year	Poltrack (1983)
Size of Sales Transaction	Fournier & Martin (1983)

[1]References do not necessarily find the same relationship between determinants and measures of economic value. Dependent variables are not uniform among these studies.

[*]Adapted from Webster and Lichty, 1991.

position of the audience. Poltrack also pointed out important pricing variations by daypart. He used the *CPM index*, a statistic that compares individual markets on the basis of the price charged to reach 1,000 viewers, as an independent variable in equations to predict station revenue. The variables that he found to be significant in the pricing equation for national spot revenue were the CPM index, and the *buying power index*, a measure of the market's economic vitality. Local advertising revenue was more dependent on competition in the marketplace, particularly competition from print media.

Fournier and Martin (1983) also looked at the effects of market variables on the price of commercial time. Although they found that audience size and composition were important factors in estimating commercial prices, they also incorporated a measure of uncertainty of audience delivery into their analysis. This measure, the variance of forecast error, had a negative relationship to the dependent variable, which means that less error translated into higher prices.

Finally, Fratrik's (1989) study of broadcast stations found that audience and market size were key predictors of advertising revenue. He used per capita income as a measure of market affluence and found the expected positive relationship between this variable and station revenue. He identified interesting differences between national/regional and local advertising revenue, including a significant and positive effect of cable penetration in the national/regional equation.

METHOD: EXPLAINING PRICE VARIATIONS IN MARKET LEVEL DATA

The study described in the following pages builds on and extends this previous work. Our dependent variable is a market level statistic—the average cost to reach 1,000 viewers in a television market. We attempt to isolate factors that contribute to intermarket variation in the price of advertising time, and to estimate the independent contribution of each variable. As demonstrated later, linear regression analysis shows that the cost of television time in individual markets is influenced by the structural characteristics of the market, the demographic makeup of the audience, and the quality of audience information that is available. The study provides evidence for the centrality of structural factors as predictors of price, and the importance of accuracy in ratings measurement. The results suggest further avenues of research that could refine our understanding of how the economic value of audiences is determined.

The unit of analysis in this study was the *designated marketing area* (DMA), a term used by the A. C. Nielsen company to define local television markets in the United States. Each DMA has different structural characteristics related to audience and media. The markets vary in size from more than 5 million households in places like New York and Los Angeles to less than 50,000 households in places like Lima and Anniston. Some markets have only one local television outlet, whereas others have more than six highly competitive stations. Unique conditions in each local television market affect advertising cost structures, and an advertiser who purchases time in the national spot market will find that prices are far from uniform across all DMAs. Market-specific efficiencies, conventionally measured by the *cost per thousand* (CPM), vary considerably—in other words, it costs more to reach 1,000 homes in some DMAs than it does in others.

The dependent variable is the average cost to reach 1,000 households in a market (the household CPM) in prime time. These CPMs were calculated from fourth quarter data reported in the December 1993 issue of *Spot Quotations and Data Reports (SQAD)*. *SQAD* is an advertising industry source that provides planning costs in individual markets. Estimates are based on historical costs in each market, adjusted for economic and other conditions that might affect the price of advertising time. Pricing data were collected for 199 television markets. It is important to note that this prime time CPM is for each market as a whole, and does not reflect pricing differences among individual television stations in a market. If a market's prime time CPM is $23.29, then an advertiser who wants to place a commercial during that time period will have to pay an average of $23.29 to reach 1,000 homes in the market. The unit cost of the commercial will depend on the size of the audience—each 1,000 homes will add, on average, $23.29 to the unit cost in that market.

Although advertising time in the national spot market is bought and sold on the basis of cost per rating point, the CPM allows useful intermarket comparisons. Unlike the *cost per point*, the CPM standardizes the base on number of households. A $10.00 CPM in Boston represents exactly the same price as a $10.00 CPM in Bangor, even though the markets differ substantially in size. But a 1 rating in Boston represents far more households than a 1 rating in Bangor, so a $100.00 cost per point in the larger market is far more efficient than a $100.00 cost per point in the smaller one. In other words, the CPM measure used in this analysis controls for audience size in order to evaluate the underlying cost efficiency of advertising time.

We chose independent variables on the basis of past research findings and new theoretical questions. Initially, we hypothesized that structural variables in each market and the composition of the potential audience would strongly affect the cost of advertising time. One relatively unexplored theoretical question that was particularly important to the analysis was the contribution that quality of ratings information makes to the cost of advertising. As discussed later, this informational characteristic was operationalized in two ways: as differences in data collection methodology;

and as the standard error of ratings estimates. For ease of explanation, these independent variables can be categorized as (a) market size/audience composition, (b) quality of audience information, and (c) competitive conditions.

Market Size/Audience Composition

Initially, there were five variables in this first category: (a) the percentage of total U.S. television homes that a market represents, (b) the percent of total market population that is 18–49 years old, (c) the retail sales per household, (d) the percentage of households using television in prime time (the *HUT level*), and (e) an index of the racial/ethnic composition of the market.

Market size was expected to have a negative correlation with the CPM. This expectation was based on the comments of buyers who anticipate lower CPMs in larger markets—in other words, more efficient buys. Audience composition variables were expected to have a positive effect on the dependent variable—the younger and more affluent the market, the more valuable the time should be to advertisers. And homes using television, or HUT, was expected to have a negative relationship to the CPM. The HUT level indicates the number of rating points available to the advertiser at any given time. For example, if the HUT is 50, then 50% of all television households in the market are watching television during prime time. This effectively places a cap on the number of rating points that are for sale in the marketplace. Higher HUT levels can be interpreted as more available audience exposures. Increasing the HUT level is tantamount to increasing the supply of these exposures, so the pressure on price should be negative. Conversely, decreasing the HUT level should exert an upward pressure on price.

The "White/non-White" variable was included in order to test whether the racial makeup of a market influences the price that advertisers are willing to pay for time. This variable is an index that compares the concentration of Whites in a given market to the national average. An index greater than 100 indicates that there is a higher concentration of Whites in the market; an index of less than 100 indicates that the relative population of Whites is less than the national average. This information was obtained from the A.C. Nielsen *DMA Test Market Profiles* (Nielsen Media Research, November, 1992). As reported there, it does not allow for very narrow segmentation of the audience. In fact, the categories are simply "Whites" and "non-Whites." The effect of this variable could be negative, meaning that advertisers would pay more to reach a more highly targeted non-White population, or it could be positive, meaning that advertisers will pay more for markets with a higher concentration of White viewers.

Quality of Audience Information

Quality of information is addressed by the incorporation of a dummy variable that differentiates metered and diary-only markets, and by the inclusion of standard error of a 10 rating in each market. The standard error is a statistic provided by Nielsen that indicates quality differences in the samples used to generate the ratings in television markets. Given the published ratings estimates, the standard error indicates the likelihood that the real rating would fall in a certain range. The viewing level of 10 was chosen somewhat arbitrarily. Nielsen provides standard error estimates for various levels of viewing, and a 10 rating is a reasonable average. The relationships found between standard error and other variables at 10 should hold at other viewing levels as well.

We expected to find that buyers will pay more for better information. In the context of the present analysis, this expectation means that there should be a positive correlation between meter methodology and CPM. The common wisdom in the industry is that meters do a much better job of capturing real viewing levels. This is because they record viewing whenever the set is actually on. In contrast, the diary methodology is subject to problems of recall—the person who fills it out generally does so after the fact, perhaps even completing the entire weekly diary on the last day of the measurement week. So, in a relative sense, meters mean higher quality data.

The willingness to pay more for better information would also be suggested by a negative correlation between standard error and CPM. This is because smaller standard errors mean better information. This does not imply, however, that individual buyers check the standard errors before deciding on a fair market price for the advertising time. The effect of the standard error is likely to show up in the post-buy analysis, which indicates how well the ratings were predicted from past program ratings. Ratings in a market with relatively high standard errors would be more difficult to predict with accuracy than ratings in a market with lower standard errors. The greater uncertainty would translate into lower prices.

Competitive Conditions

Competitive conditions are captured by the number of stations in the market and the cable penetration. It was expected that vigorous competition in markets with many stations would have the effect of lowering prices for the advertiser. The effect of cable penetration, on the other hand, seems more open to question. Some studies have found a positive correlation between cost and cable penetration (e.g., Fratrik, 1989), but an argument could be made for a negative correlation as well. The positive correlation would show up if cable were simply siphoning off viewers from broadcast audiences and not giving advertisers the possibility of buying time to reach those audiences (Wirth & Bloch, 1985). The negative correlation would be present if advertisers could substitute cable commercials for broadcast commercials. Under this scenario, cable would represent increased competition in the market.

Another reason that the effect of cable is difficult to predict is that the competitive status of cable vis-à-vis the broadcaster in the national spot market has changed in recent years. Although the system is still developing, advertisers who wish to place national or regional buys on cable systems can work through cable rep firms in the same way that they work through broadcast rep firms to place advertising on individual stations. This makes cable a potential competitor for national spot dollars, and could have an important effect on how broadcast advertising time is priced (Phalen, 1996).

Table 3.2 provides summary definitions for all variables and reports the simple correlations among them. The natural log of the dependent variable was used in the regression equations. The relationships between CPM and the predictor variables were not always in the expected directions, or, as in the case of market size, they were in the expected direction but not significant. The concentration of younger viewers was positively related to the CPM. In other words, advertisers will pay more to reach a younger audience than an older audience. The HUT level was negatively correlated with CPM. As the supply of rating points goes up, the cost of those rating points goes down. Retail sales per household was positively related (at the .10 significance level) to the CPM, which means that advertisers are willing to pay more for affluent viewers. These correlations indicate that there are important characteristics of the audience, measured in the aggregate, that influence the price of advertising time.

It was somewhat unexpected that the simple correlation between the meter dummy and CPM was not significant. One possible reason for this is that the small number of metered markets in the analysis (only 29) means that significance would be difficult to achieve. Another possible reason is that the true correlation is being masked by collinearity problems. In fact, when we controlled for other variables in the equation the effect of meters was positive and significant. The quality of information, captured by the standard error, showed an unexpected positive correlation with CPM. Because lower standard errors suggest better information, this correlation was surprising. We added the square of standard error to the regression equation in order to test whether the true relationship might be curvilinear. This will be further discussed in the following section.

Cable penetration had a significant and positive correlation with the dependent variable. This seems to indicate that cable is not yet a serious competitor in the national spot market. This positive relationship held even

TABLE 3.2
Correlation Matrix for Determinants of Audience Prices

Variables	2	3	4	5	6	7	8	9	10	11
Dependent Variable										
1. Market CPM	-.08	.18*	-.24*	.14	-.05	.02	.56*	.60*	.31*	-.12
Market Size/Audience Composition										
2. Percent of TVHH		.31*	.36*	.28*	-.14	.66*	-.53*	-.49*	-.12	.76*
3. Percent of 18 to 49			-.15*	.49*	-.20*	.33*	-.28*	-.26*	-.07	.46*
4. HUT level				-.05	-.07	.53*	-.30*	-.28*	-.01	.37*
5. Retail sales					-.11	.31*	-.29*	-.28*	.11	.42*
6. White/Non-White						-.07	-.04	-.07	.00	-.16*
Quality of Audience Information										
7. Meter versus diary							-.45*	-.42*	-.14*	.73*
8. Standard Error (SE)								.99*	.18*	-.63*
9. Square of SE									.19*	-.60*
Competitive Conditions										
10. Cable penetration										-.13
11. Television stations										

Note: Variables are defined as follows:

1. Natural log of cost per thousand viewing households in a market.
2. The percent of total U.S. TV Households in a market.
3. The percent of total market population between the ages of 18 and 49.
4. "Homes Using Television," the percent of all TV Households watching during prime time.
5. The per household retail sales in the market.
6. Index to the national average total White population.
7. Dummy variable, coded 1 for metered market, 0 for diary-only market.
8. Standard error at a 10 rating.
9. The square of the standard error at a 10 rating.
10. The percent of cable penetration in the market.
11. The total number of television stations in the market.

*Correlation significant at $p < .05$

TABLE 3.3
Determinants of Audience Prices

Variables	Beta Coefficients	T Value
Market Size/Audience Composition		
Percent 18 to 49	0.197	3.513*
HUT level	-0.184	-3.141*
Retail sales	0.113	2.128*
"White/Non-White"	0.111	2.402*
Quality of Audience Information		
Meter versus diary	0.289	4.501*
Standard error (SE)	-1.634	-4.022*
Square of SE	2.344	5.846*
Competitive Conditions		
Cable penetration	0.194	4.214*

All Markets ($n = 199$). Adjusted R Square = .63. *T value significant $p < .05$

when we controlled for the other independent variables. Rather than increasing the supply of audience exposures available to the advertiser, cable decreases it by taking viewership from the broadcast stations. Another measure of competition, the number of stations in the market, was negatively correlated with CPM (at the .10 significance level). This relationship was expected because more stations means more competition, which generally results in lower prices for the advertiser.

One of the highest simple correlations between independent variables in this study was between the total number of stations and market size. In fact, the number of stations was also highly correlated with several other variables in the analysis. It showed high positive correlations with per household buying income and the meter dummy, and it was negatively correlated with the standard error.

The results of the multiple regression analysis are presented in Table 3.3. The standardized beta coefficients are shown to illustrate the relative effects of these variables on price. All variables were entered into the equation rather than selected out, as they would be in a stepwise regression. Two variables, size of market, and number of stations, were eliminated from the final equation. The size of market was not a significant variable in explaining variation in the CPM. Its significance level was only .43 when it was added to the equation. Its inclusion did not substantially affect the R^2, nor did it alter the coefficients of the other variables in any substantive way. The same was true of the number of stations in the market. This variable did not help the R^2, nor was it significant as part of the multiple regression. Part of the problem with this variable is its high correlation with the other independent variables.

These results demonstrate that variation in the price of advertising time among different markets can be largely accounted for by differences in structural characteristics. Price is a function of the size and demographic composition of the potential audience, the characteristics of audience measurement in the market, as well as certain competitive characteristics of the marketplace. In fact, 63% of the variation in intermarket CPM was explained by these independent variables. In general, advertisers are willing to pay more for audiences that are younger, more affluent, and, as indicated by the results of the meter variable, can be predicted with greater accuracy. They pay more for audiences in markets where the supply of available rating points is constrained in some way, and there is some evidence that they pay more for advertising in markets with a higher concentration of White viewers.

Although it is difficult to isolate the effect of the quality of information on the cost of advertising time, this analysis suggests that there is a relationship. The positive coefficient on the meter dummy in the equation is perhaps the most obvious indication that research methodology influences price. Advertisers are willing to pay more in markets where the meter is used for data collection.

The effect of standard error on price needs further investigation. The significance of the squared standard error indicates that there is a curvilinear relationship between this measure of information quality and the dependent variable. Preliminary analysis shows that the relationship between CPM and standard error is likely to be negative (the higher the standard error, the lower the price) at lower standard error levels. At higher standard error levels the relationship becomes positive (higher standard error, higher price). This result is unexpected, but there are at least two possible explanations for it. One is that high standard errors would make it more difficult to predict future ratings with accuracy. This situation could make it necessary for the station to give away a large number of make goods to compensate for audience shortfalls. In anticipation of this, stations might hold back more inventory so that there is less time available for sale. The resulting decrease in supply would raise the price of time relative to those markets where the predicted ratings come pretty close to the actual ratings.

The second possible reason for this relationship has more to do with diary measurement than with standard error per se. The higher standard error levels are in the smaller markets, and the smaller markets are measured with diary methodology. On average, the prime time HUT levels in diary markets are lower than in metered markets. This means a lower supply of rating points, which might have the overall effect of raising advertising rates. Additional research is necessary to explore these relationships.

The final category of independent variable, competitive conditions, also represents an area for future research. As local cable systems become more adept at selling their audiences in the national spot market (see Phalen, 1996), the impact of cable penetration on price is likely to change. It will be interesting to see over the next several years whether large regional and national advertisers do turn to local cable as a substitute for broadcast time. If this happens, cable penetration should begin to show a negative effect on market price.

DISCUSSION: THE MASS AUDIENCE
AS A COMMODITY

In the advertising marketplace, the television audience is bought and sold in much the same way as commodities in other markets. Although several factors, most notably the sheer number of viewers, affect its value to advertisers, the market price of this commodity is ultimately determined by the laws of supply and demand. The study presented here controlled for audience size and demonstrated that there are structural explanations for differences in the cost of advertising time across markets, including competition in the market and quality of available audience information.

In a larger sense, the commodification of audiences should enrich our understanding of the mass audience concept. In this arena, more than any other, viewers lose their individual identities. They become part of a larger entity. They are counted up and sold as "gross rating points," a practice that has the effect of highlighting the absolute number of people in attendance. They are categorized into groups and priced at some "cost per thousand." At first blush, this all seems rather dehumanizing.

But we can know the human condition in different ways. The practice of seeing the audience as a mass persists because it offers a useful perspective. For the advertiser, of course, it is the opening wedge in inducing large numbers of people to buy a particular product or service. For the politician, it could be a way to fathom public opinion or manage a program of social reform. For the programmer, it may be a tool to gauge the dimensions and demands of popular culture. It allows us to see something of society that might otherwise elude our notice. It is method of knowing.

Recently, it has become popular to proclaim that the idea of a mass audience has outlived its usefulness in industry and academe. Much of the rationale for this death sentence comes from what critics see as changes in the advertising marketplace. Advertisers, it is said, are no longer interested in reaching a mass market. Instead, each wants highly targeted segments of the population defined by some combination of "geo-demographics," product purchase histories, and lifestyles. At the extreme, proponents of direct marketing advocate sending each consumer a specially tailored advertising message, bypassing mass media altogether.

It is true that advertisers are increasingly concerned about the efficiency of their media buys. In fact, they use the term "wasted exposures" to refer to the effect of commercial time placed in programs that may attract large audiences that contain relatively few potential customers. Moreover, they have prevailed on audience measurement firms to sharpen their ability to describe audiences so these inefficiences can be assessed (Barnes & Thomson, 1994; Larson, 1992). It is also true that the media have responded to advertiser demands by offering more specialized content. This has fragmented the audience, and in some cases, produced a more demographically uniform commodity for sale (Barnes, 1990). These are all real, probably irreversible, changes in the media environment that we consider in some detail in chapter 7.

All this notwithstanding, when confronted with obituaries on the mass audience we are reminded of Mark Twain's famous quote that the rumors of his death were "greatly exaggerated." As we pointed out in chapter 1, there is nothing about the growing interest in market segments that alters the fundamental attributes of mass audience thinking. People are still reduced to a few defining characteristics, counted up, and sold. It is a fallacy to believe that these practices produce anything other than a mass audience. In fact, even the most highly targeted national network audiences are likely to number in the millions. Furthermore, many advertisers still seek to reach a vast, heterogeneous market. They pay a premium for highly rated network programs in order to guarantee the reach of their campaigns. Or, they simply reconstitute a mass audience by buying many small blocks of viewers, all the while devising strategies for "beating fragmentation." In light of all this, we suspect mass audiences will be a staple of the media industry well into the next century.

Chapter 4

Inheritance Effects

Inheritance effects are one of the most pervasive features of television audience behavior. Sometimes called lead-in effects, or simply audience flow, they are the inordinately high levels of audience duplication found between adjacent television programs. Inheritance effects are at the heart of many programming practices. They are also an essential element in various attempts to model mass audience behavior. Anyone who wants to know how television audiences form and change over time must understand inheritance effects.

Since the early 1960s, media researchers have reported inheritance effects between consecutively scheduled network programs (Kirsch & Banks, 1962). Almost without exception, the audience for one television program is overrepresented in the audience of the program that immediately follows. This phenomenon of audience behavior seems a logical consequence of offering viewers a succession of programs designed to retain audiences from one program to the next. Yet, most research up through the 1970s suggested that this feature of audience duplication was unaffected by program content. Considering the heavy emphasis that audience theory placed on program type preferences, this was a troublesome nonresult.

In the 1980s a number of studies were done in an effort to better understand inheritance effects. This chapter reviews the relevant research and reports the results of one study in particular detail (Webster, 1985). It is intended to clarify the determinants of inheritance effects and place the phenomenon in the theoretical framework developed in chapter 2.

Inheritance effects are one of three well-documented patterns of cumulative audience behavior. The other two are repeat viewing, a predictable day-to-day duplication of audiences across programs in a series (Goodhardt et al., 1987; Webster & Wang, 1992), and channel loyalty, a disproportionately high duplication of audiences for any pair of programs broadcast on the same network (Bruno, 1973; Goodhardt et al., 1987; Headen, Klompmaker, & Rust, 1979). Despite certain differences in nomenclature and methods of reporting, each of these patterns identifies some special tendency for the audience of one program to be represented in the audience of another. In the case of inheritance effects, the programs are scheduled back-to-back on the same channel. Although this might be conceptualized as a kind of channel loyalty, it is usually treated as a unique feature of audience behavior because adjacent program audience duplication routinely exceeds the levels predicted under an assumption of ordinary channel loyalty (Goodhardt et al., 1987).

THE DUPLICATION OF VIEWING LAW

Among the analytical techniques commonly used to assess such patterns of program audience duplication, perhaps the most straightforward is the method developed by Goodhardt et al. (1987). Referred to as the duplication of viewing law, it states the percentage of all viewers who see two programs broadcast by the same network on different days (r_{st}) is a function of the rating of one program (r_s) multiplied by the rating of the other program (r_t) multiplied by some constant (k) divided by 100 (i.e., $r_{st} = r_s r_t k / 100$). Under this formulation, when $k = 1$, the equation defines a condition of stochastic independence between program audiences. Goodhardt and Ehrenberg (1969) argued that, to the extent the constant (k) must be increased to predict observed levels of duplication (r_{st}), this formula served as an index of channel loyalty.

In practice, the value of the constant (k) for U.S. networks has been estimated to be approximately 1.6, meaning that viewers of one network program are "about 60% more likely to watch another programme on the same channel on another day than is the public in general" (Goodhardt et al., 1987, p. 82). For channels in the United Kingdom, values of the constant tend to be slightly higher. Such indices of channel loyalty have been applied to network programs broadcast on the same day to demonstrate that adjacent and next-to-adjacent programs exhibit the special case of channel loyalty commonly called inheritance effects. Goodhardt et al. (1987) speculated that these especially high levels of audience duplication result from: (a) people staying tuned out of inertia, (b) noncoterminous programming, or (c) people tuning to the earlier program to wait for the next scheduled program (i.e., a *lead-out effect*).

Beyond documenting the existence of these features of audience flow, the work of Goodhardt et al. (1975, 1987) is noteworthy for its failure to find any program-type effects. As we noted in our review of audience behavior in chapter 2, a considerable body of theory holds that preferences for program content should be the principle determinant of program choice. Theoretically, then, one would expect to find a kind of program-type loyalty wherein audience duplication is predicted by similarities in program content (Webster & Wakshlag, 1982). Yet Goodhardt et al. reported no special tendency for the viewer of one program to watch another program of the same type. Instead, all readily observable patterns of audience duplication seem to be predicted by scheduling characteristics alone.

Noting this counterintuitive result, Headen et al. (1979) argued that the duplication of viewing law was analytically problematic. They proposed a method of analysis through which the influence of program type on levels of duplication could be more precisely determined. Thus, they were able to demonstrate that program type did play a significant, if modest, role in predicting audience duplication across programs broadcast on different days, and concluded that patterns of duplication in the United States were considerably more complex than those in the United Kingdom. For a particularly thoughtful discussion of the duplication of viewing law and the analytical alternatives, the reader should see Henriksen (1985).

Despite some progress in describing the scope of inheritance effects, they have remained a little understood feature of audience behavior. Why do they exist? To what extent do program and scheduling characteristics contribute to their emergence? In 1985, Webster used a predecessor of the audience model presented in chapter 2 (i.e., Webster & Wakshlag, 1983) to investigate these questions.

DETERMINANTS OF AUDIENCE INHERITANCE

The reader will recall that, in chapter 2, we identified four broad determinants of audience behavior. This study of inheritance effects investigated representatives from three of those four categories. The impact of audience structure was addressed by considering how patterns of audience availability might determine inheritance effects. The structure of the media was examined by considering the impact of scheduling variables on patterns of audience duplication. Consistent with our earlier discussion of individual level audience factors, and the concerns raised by Headen et al. (1979), we also assessed the impact of program content on audience inheritance. We discuss each of these factors in turn.

It has been argued that underlying patterns of audience availability, which are typically unaffected by the schedule of programs, produce highly correlated patterns of television use (Gensch & Shaman, 1980; Webster & Wakshlag, 1983). These patterns of television use are, in turn, largely responsible for the existence of structurally defined patterns of audience flow. Analyses of channel loyalty and repeat viewing tend to confirm this explanation (Barwise, Ehrenberg, & Goodhardt, 1982; Goodhardt et al., 1987; Webster & Wang, 1992). In the case of inheritance effects, then, the most likely explanation for high levels of program audience duplication is that, on a given evening, the same people tend to be available and to watch television in adjacent time periods. These are the general patterns of total audience overlap we described in chapter 2, and could account for the overall emergence of inheritance effects in adjacent or next-to-adjacent programs.

Unfortunately, a precise determination of how audience availability contributes to program audience duplication is tricky. If the analysis is confined to adjacent programs, then the levels of total audience overlap across those time periods, although relatively high, would be expected to demonstrate little variability. It would simply appear to be a constant in the background. On the other hand, seeking increased variation in total audience overlap by extending the analysis to more widely separated time periods is still problematic. Although it can be argued that such levels of audience overlap are random with respect to available content (e.g., Barwise et al., 1982; Rust et al., 1992; Webster & Wakshlag, 1983), total audiences are nonetheless the sum of individual program audiences. The two constructs (i.e., program audience and total TV audience) although theoretically distinct, are empirically confounded. As a result, using total audience overlap to predict program audience duplication produces an artificially high correlation.

In a preliminary analysis reported later in the chapter, this research explored underlying patterns of audience overlap by examining the extent to which the same people watch television in adjacent and more widely separated evening hours. It is left to the reader to decide whether such patterns constitute a plausible explanation for the general phenomenon of inheritance effects. In this framework of audience availability, however, the effect of additional variables can be examined more precisely.

The structure of the media, especially the juxtaposition of programs, is known to affect the formation of audiences. Prime time scheduling strategies are such that not all programs begin and end at the same time. As a result, viewers of a program that has just ended may have only one choice for continued viewing among the major networks, unless they decide to begin watching a program midstream on another channel. Although such behavior undoubtedly does occur, it would seem as the number of choices available to viewers decreases, inheritance effects would increase. Consequently, this research posits an inverse relationship between audience size and the number of shows beginning at the interface of the programs in question. Later in this chapter, we touch on how this factor may or may not be complicated by the numerical abundance of the new media.

As noted in chapter 2, several strains of audience theory, including economic models of program choice (e.g., Owen & Wildman, 1992), gratificationist theory (e.g., Rosengren et al., 1985) and marketing models (Rust et al., 1992), identify program-type preferences as a primary determinant of program choice. It is widely believed that viewers have clear and enduring preferences for specific content characteristics or types of programs and, as a result, will tend to watch those programs when they are available (e.g.,

Bowman & Farley, 1972; Lehmann, 1971). This notion seems consistent with the approach taken by programmers intent on developing a cohesive lineup of shows for the evening schedule (Eastman, 1993). If programs of the same type are broadcast by a network in adjacent time periods, one would expect increased inheritance effects. Conversely, if a competitor offers a channel's viewers an opportunity to see another program of the same type, inheritance effects might be diminished.

Here too, however, an analysis presents certain difficulties. First, there is the problem of the appropriate program typology. As noted in chapter 2, the theoretical standard for a typology is that it be defined in terms of viewer preferences. To the extent that such types exist, they appear to correspond to conventional industry program categories (e.g., situation comedies, action drama, news, etc.). Second, in the context of audience inheritance, there is a potential problem of *saturation effects* (Lehmann, 1971). Even if viewers tend to like programs of a type, how many consecutive showings will it take before fans of that genre are satiated? It seems likely that a successful programmer must orchestrate variations on a theme in evening programming, a theme that may transcend conventional typologies. Third, program types are typically confounded with scheduling characteristics, making it difficult to attribute whatever patterns are found to one variable or the other (Webster & Wakshlag, 1983). Although multivariate statistics can help to sort this out with data from the field, a certain amount of confounding is inescapable. Despite these difficulties, this research hypothesizes that: (a) audience duplication will increase when a program is followed immediately by another program of the same type on the same channel, and (b) audience duplication will decrease when a program is followed immediately by another program of the same type on a different channel.

Finally, to empirically assess the determinants of audience inheritance, it is necessary to consider exactly how these effects should be quantified. Generally, audience duplication or overlap has been expressed in one of two ways. First, as is the case with the duplication of viewing law and related models, it has been defined as the proportion of the entire audience that sees any pair of programs. Such proportions are readily interpretable as *absolute measures* of audience size and may be of particular use to media planners and time buyers. Second, audience duplication is sometimes defined as the percentage of one program's audience that also watches another program. This method of reporting audience duplication is typical in analyses of repeat viewing (e.g., Barwise et al., 1982; Webster & Wang, 1992) and audience availability (e.g., Aske, 1978; Barwise & Ehrenberg, 1988). In fact, researchers at Aske, Ltd. have used such an approach to analyze inheritance effects, reporting that about 50% of one program's audience sees the following program (Aske, 1980). Unlike the absolute measures of audience duplication, such *relative measures* of overlap tend to be insensitive to the ratings of the programs involved in the pairings.

Although neither measure seems uniformly superior to the other, to be consistent with the majority of research, this study used the first measure of absolute audience duplication (i.e., r_{st}) as the dependent variable in the main regression analysis reported later in the chapter. Where it is useful for purposes of comparison to other analyses of audience overlap (e.g., Table 4.1), the relative measure is reported.

An important consequence of using audience duplication as the dependent variable is that program ratings will almost certainly be a statistically powerful predictor variable. Not surprisingly, highly rated programs will, even under an assumption of statistical independence, have relatively large duplicated audiences. In practice, it is the cross product of program ratings (i.e., $r_s r_t$) that has been used to predict levels of duplication (Goodhardt et al., 1987; Headen et al., 1979). In the present context, however, there is an advantage in allowing each program rating to predict duplication independently. Because the programs in an adjacent pair are temporally ordered, determining what program's rating is a better predictor of duplication could illuminate the relative importance of lead-in versus lead-out effects (Henriksen, 1985).

METHOD: CUMULATIVE MEASURES
FROM INDIVIDUAL LEVEL DATA

Webster and Lichty (1991) noted that there are two broad categories of mass audience analysis: cumulative, which tracks the behavior of individuals over time, and gross, which provides a discrete snapshot of audience size at one or more times. Because inheritance effects are about how audiences flow and change membership over time, quantifying the effect requires a cumulative form of analysis. In other words, the data must tell us what each individual is watching in different time periods. There are several examples of this type of analysis in the literature (e.g., Goodhardt et al., 1987; Headen et al., 1979; Henriksen, 1985; Rust et al., 1992; Webster, 1985). The data reported here are of this sort.

We might note in passing that cumulative analyses based on individual level data are not the only way that researchers have assessed inheritance effects. Many studies have explored inheritance effects using gross measures of the audience (e.g., Boemer, 1987; Cooper, 1993; Tiedge & Ksobiech, 1986; Walker, 1988; Webster & Newton, 1988). In effect, these studies determine how the size of a program's audience is related to the size of the preceding program audience. This form of analysis can certainly offer valuable information to programmers and scholars alike. It can also support and extend the results suggested by cumulative analyses. But, strictly speaking, it provides only circumstantial evidence of the effect in question.

The results reported in this chapter are based on Arbitron television diary data collected in February 1982 in the Portland, Maine *Area of Dominant Influence* (ADI). The Portland market, which had three VHF network affiliates and no other commercial stations, was selected because it afforded an opportunity to examine viewer behaviors in an environment uncomplicated by local independents or UHF "handicaps." From the original sample of 1,463 persons represented in four independent weekly samples, a subset of all female heads of households ($N= 500$) was used in the analysis. This step was taken to eliminate correlations among individuals living in the same household that might weight results in the direction of larger families.

As suggested earlier, audience overlap is reported as the percentage of viewers watching television at one time who also watched at a later time that evening. This is the method of reporting used in the preliminary analysis of audience availability. Otherwise, the dependent measure of audience duplication is the percentage of the total population that watched any pair of adjacent programs (r_{st}). This procedure is similar to the one employed by Headen et al. (1979). Purists may be interested in noting that, for purposes of estimation, Headen et al. used a logarithmic transformation of r_{st} and $r_s r_t$. In the data reported here, the transformation of r_{st}, r_s, and r_t was necessary to avoid violating the assumptions that underlie the linear model (Bauer & Fink, 1983). The symbol *ln* is used to denote the natural logarithm of each variable.

Program pairs were treated as cases in the main correlational analyses. Programs in each pair were scheduled back to back on the same evening and on the same channel. The analysis included all such pairings from 7:00 p.m. to 10:30 p.m. (EST), Monday through Sunday. Some program pairs were eliminated, as the aggregation of four weeks' viewing became uninterpretable due to scheduling changes during the ratings period. In all, 74 program pairs were included in the analysis.

Five predictor variables were used to develop a multiple regression equation: (a) the rating of the earlier program in each pair (rating 1), (b) the rating of the later program in each pair (rating 2), (c) the number of network programs beginning at the end of the first program in the pair (choices), which could assume a value ranging from 1–3, (d) the within-channel (WI) program type, coded 1 when both programs in the pair were of the same type, and 0 when they were different types, and (e) across-channel (AC) program type, coded 1 if a competing channel scheduled a program of the same type at the end of the first program in the pair, and 0 if it did not. The equation was estimated stepwise to explore the relative contributions of each variable.

TABLE 4.1
Overlap of Within-Day Prime Time Television Audiences

Days	Of Those Who Watched Television at 7:00 P.M. the Percentage of Those Who Also Watched At:		
	8:00 P.M.	9:00 P.M.	10:00 P.M.
Monday	78.1%	74.5%	56.3%
Tuesday	77.4%	66.9%	46.4%
Wednesday	72.8%	62.8%	52.5%
Thursday	69.8%	63.0%	44.2%
Friday	75.0%	62.7%	43.4%
Saturday	67.9%	66.0%	49.8%
Sunday	80.1%	72.3%	58.7%
Average	74.4%	66.9%	50.2%

The results are presented in two parts. The first explores underlying patterns of audience availability, or more properly, total television use (Table 4.1). The second reports the results of the regression analysis (Tables 4.2 and 4.3).

The first table summarized the overall pattern of television audience overlap for adjacent and more widely separated evening hours. On average, 74.4% of those who watched television at 7:00 p.m. also watched at 8:00 p.m. On each night, total audience overlap decreased as the evening progressed. By 10:00 p.m., only half of the early evening viewers were still in the audience. This 50% level of audience overlap is quite similar to the 53% level of day-to-day repeat viewing reported for prime time audiences in the United States (Headen et al., 1979). As expected, total audience overlap across all pairs of adjacent programs (sometimes only a half hour apart) was high ($M = 80.7\%$) and demonstrated relatively little variability ($SD = 8.0$).

This pattern of total audience overlap seems to explain the presence of inheritance effects between adjacent or next-to-adjacent programs. It is simply a program-specific manifestation of the general tendency for an unusually high percentage of the same viewers to be watching television in adjacent or next-to-adjacent time periods. Evening programs scheduled more than 2 hours apart exist in a framework of total audience overlap that is essentially the same as that found on a day-to-day basis. It is not surprising, then, that duplicated audiences would not deviate substantially from levels predicted by ordinary channel loyalty.

Table 4.2 presents a correlation matrix of the variables used in the multiple regression. As expected, the number of choices available to viewers at the interface between two programs is inversely related to the size of the duplicated audience. This result has been confirmed in subsequent analyses using gross measures of the audience over a period of years (Tiedge & Ksobiech, 1986; Walker, 1988). Furthermore, there is the expected confounding of program type and scheduling characteristics, as reflected in the correlations between program-type variables and choices. Overall, however, these correlations do not seem large enough to present serious problems of multicollinearity. They are discussed in greater detail at the end of the chapter.

Table 4.3 summarizes the results of the stepwise regression. Consistent with other analyses of day-to-day audience duplication (Headen et al., 1979; Henriksen, 1985), the ratings of the individual programs were significant predictors of their duplicated audience. Among adjacent program pairs, however, the size of the earlier program's rating played a much greater role in determining duplicated audience size ($R^2=.68$). That factor, in combination with the number of choices, explained over 80% of the variance in audience duplication ($R^2=.81$). The rating of the second program and within channel program type entered the equation on the third and fourth steps and resulted in modest, yet significant, improvements in the explanatory power of the final equation ($R^2=.85$). Across channel program type did not add significantly to this four-variable model and was omitted from the equation.

Stated in terms of the relative measures that de-emphasize the effect of program ratings, the results can be summarized as follows. About half of

TABLE 4.2
Correlation Matrix for Determinants of Audience Duplication

Variables	2	3	4	5	6
1. Duplication	.83	.38	-.39	.43	.10
2. Rating 1		.34	-.03	.21	.19
3. Rating 2			.14	-.08	.22
4. Choices				-.46	.27
5. Program Type (WI)					-.04
6. Program Type (AC)					

Note. Variables are defined as follows:
1. $ln(r_{st})$, where r_{st} is the percentage of the population seeing two programs in an adjacent pair.
2. $ln(r_s)$, where r_s is the percentage of the population seeing the earlier of the programs in an adjacent pair.
3. $ln(r_t)$, where r_t is the percentage of the population seeing the later of the programs in an adjacent pair.
4. The number of program choices available, ranging from 1 to 3.
5. Within channel program type, coded 1 if both programs were of the same type, or 0 if of different types.
6. Across channel program type, coded 1 if the same type was available, or 0 if the same type was unavailable on competing channels.

TABLE 4.3
Determinants of Audience Duplication Between Adjacent Network Programs[a]

Independent Variables	Unstandardized Coefficients (F value)[b]			
	Step 1	Step 2	Step 3	Step 4
Rating 1 $ln(r_s)$	1.066 (153.04)	1.051 (246.52)	.972 (215.03)	.928 (203.86)
Choices		-.261 (48.47)	-.280 (63.12)	-.233 (38.34)
Rating 2 $ln(r_t)$			.212 (12.18)	.288 (15.32)
Program Type (WI)				.166 (7.93)
Constant	-.91	-.21	-.46	-.59
R^2	.68	.81	.84	.85
Overall F	153.04[c]	151.22[c]	120.75[c]	101.51[c]
df	1, 72	2, 71	3, 70	4, 69

[a]Dependent variable is in the form $ln(r_{st})$. [b]All figures in parentheses are F values significant at $p < .001$. [c]Each overall F value was significant at $p < .001$. All incremental Fs were significant at $p < .01$.

those who viewed one program also viewed the following program ($M = 49.0\%$, $SD = 15.6$). This is an average level of audience inheritance virtually identical to that reported by researchers at Aske (1980). However, the grand average masks the considerable influence exerted by the number of choices available to viewers at a given point in time. Under conditions where only one choice was available, the average level of inherited audience was 70.0%.

DISCUSSION: STABILITY AND PREDICTION

This study, as well as many others we cited, is a testament to the stability and pervasiveness of inheritance effects. Similar results have been reported across different countries, different media systems, and different decades. It also demonstrates the tractable nature of mass behavior. Even though the actions of individual viewers may be motivated by a multitude of things, in the aggregate they reveal predictable patterns.

The findings clearly suggest that the overall phenomenon of inheritance effects results from underlying patterns of total audience overlap. Adjacent network programs share a high number of viewers because a high number of the same people tend to be watching television in adjacent time periods. This finding is consistent with the broader assertion that structurally defined patterns of audience flow are attributable, at least in part, to patterns of viewer availability (Webster & Wakshlag, 1983).

Other factors, however, exercise a significant influence on the extent of audience duplication between any pair of adjacent programs. As with studies of day-to-day audience duplication (Goodhardt et al., 1987), the ratings of the programs involved in the pairing affected the absolute size of the duplicated audience. Among adjacent programs, the earlier program's rating is an especially powerful predictor. This finding is not unique to U.S. audiences. Henriksen (1985) reported a similar result based on an analysis of Danish television viewers. A fuller explanation of why this occurs must await investigations that allow causal inference. Nevertheless, this finding suggests that inheritance effects are more a matter of audience lead-in than lead-out. That is, viewers tend to see a later program because they have watched its predecessor.

As Webster and Wakshlag (1983) observed, and as the present analysis indicates, program type and scheduling characteristics are correlated. Under such circumstances, sorting out which factor accounts for a given portion of the variance is difficult. For example, in all but a single, one-choice situation, programs of the same type were scheduled back-to-back. A comparison of similar type-to-type scheduling in three-choice situations and the order in which these variables were selected in the equation suggests that the number of choices is a better predictor of inheritance. This procedure, however, may have "robbed" some variance rightly attributable to program type. In fact, a small change in error variation might have reversed the order in which these variables entered the equation.

Statistical niceties aside, the impact of program content may have been further minimized by the use of a conventional industry typology. It has been argued that such schemes are overly broad and insensitive to subtle, although important, content distinctions (Greenberg & Barnett, 1971). For those inclined to believe that some programs of a type are more alike than others, the data contain reassuring glimpses of the importance of program content. For example, *Laverne and Shirley* inherited 84.2% of the audience for *Happy Days*, a level of duplication considerably higher than that of comparably scheduled program pairs. Produced by Garry Marshall, one program was a "spin-off" of the other. If ever there were two programs of a type, this pair would qualify.

The inadequacies of the program typology, combined with the mediating influences we discussed in chapter 2 (e.g., awareness, group viewing) may account for the relatively weak contributions of program-type variables, as well as the unexplained variance in the final equation. But even under more favorable circumstances, it seems unlikely that program type preferences would be a powerful predictor of audience flow. Analysts who want to know how the audience for a program is actually formed would do well to go beyond needs and preferences to consider the impact of audience availabilities and the structure of program options.

Despite the stability of these phenomena, we should not assume that they are impervious to change. There has been much speculation that the new media environment, with its abundance of choices, might alter the rules of the game (Cooper, 1996). In theory, a large number of channels coupled with remote control devices could affect the nature of audience flow. Certainly *video on demand* could strengthen the relationship between preference and choice. But there is often a considerable distance between theoretical possibilities and audience habits. Walker (1988) examined inheritance effects in more recent years and has found little evidence of significant changes. Similarly, Eastman and Newton (1995) concluded that "concerns about radical changes in viewing behavior resulting from remote control use may be overblown" (p. 77). Although the situation bears watching, we suspect inheritance effects, much as they are described in this chapter, will be with us for a long time to come.

Chapter 5

Repeat Viewing

Repeat viewing is yet another form of audience duplication. Unlike inheritance effects, which focus on audience flow between adjacent programs, repeat viewing addresses the extent to which people return to watch a program over a period of days or weeks. It is the elemental audience behavior that underlies many models of audience accumulation (Barwise, 1986; Webster & Lichty, 1991). An appreciation of repeat viewing, therefore, is relevant not only to those who produce and program television, but to a more general understanding of media reach and the frequency of exposure.

Repeat viewing has been the topic of occasional research for more than 20 years. Until the late 1980s, these studies suggested that repeat viewing was one of the more commonplace and stable of all television audience behaviors. As Goodhardt et al. (1987) noted:

> The overall result is simple if perhaps surprising. For popular programmes only around one half—generally some 55%—of the people who see a regular programme one week also see the next episode of it in the following week. This was first noted in the UK in the late sixties. But it still remains true 20 years later and it also holds in the USA and other countries. (p. 51)

This norm of audience duplication offered programmers a yardstick for measuring program loyalty. More importantly, it allowed marketers to use simple models of reach and frequency to craft their media plans. By the end of the 1980s, however, dramatic changes in the television viewing environment and a new regime of commercial audience measurement combined to complicate what had once appeared to be a straightforward feature of audience behavior.

This chapter offers an analysis of levels of repeat viewing for network series television as measured by peoplemeters. Based, in part, on a study by Webster and Wang (1992), it is intended to clarify current levels of repeat viewing and identify those factors that contribute to variation in this phenomenon. In keeping with the theme of the book, it is a study of mass behavior. It is not intended to shed light on the psychological gratifications of repeated exposure to content (e.g., Tannenbaum, 1985). Before going to a review of the literature, it is important to become familiar with *double jeopardy effects*—a more general feature of mass behavior that has significant implications for repeat viewing.

THE LAW OF DOUBLE JEOPARDY

Double jeopardy is a phenomenon of mass behavior that was first described in the academic literature by McPhee (1963). Industry researchers alerted McPhee to an odd, but persistent result in their analyses of popularity. They had discovered that among any set of media offerings (e.g., books, films, radio personalities), the less well-known options also tended to be less well-liked, even among those familiar with all the options. McPhee (1963) himself noted, "This seems absurd. The number of other people who have not yet become familiar with an alternative should have nothing to do with whether or not those who have become familiar with it like it" (p. 133). But the phenomenon has proven to be remarkably persistent and applicable to a broad range of cases in media and marketing. Writing almost 30 years after McPhee's first work on the subject, Ehrenberg, Goodhardt, and Barwise (1990) described double jeopardy as "a little-known but widely occurring and theoretically supported regularity in competitive markets" (p. 82).

In the case of audience behavior, double jeopardy has manifested itself in the form of positive correlations between measures of audience size and loyalty (e.g., repeat viewing, time spent viewing a channel, etc.). In other words, unpopular programs or channels are observed to have the double problem of both relatively few and relatively irregular viewers. This feature of mass audience behavior directly contradicts popular notions of the "small but loyal" audience. Despite its counterintuitive nature, double jeopardy effects crop up time and again. Barwise and Ehrenberg (1988) reported that television stations with a small audience reach receive only scant attention from the few who bother to tune in. They then assert that the relationship between reach and time spent viewing is so predictable that it can be fitted to a simple equation. Even among major market radio stations, which generally try to capture a small but dedicated subset of listeners, about the best that can be said is that there is no correlation between audience size and time spent listening (Barnes, 1990).

Theoretical explanations of such phenomena have tended to be statistical or probabilistic in nature. To the extent that causal relationships can be specified, it appears popularity (i.e., ratings) causes loyalty (i.e., repeat viewing; Ehrenberg et al., 1990). Like other analyses of the mass audience, empirical demonstrations of double jeopardy have relied on aggregate measures of behavior rather than individual declarations of preference. In any event, it is important to be cognizant of double jeopardy in the discussion that follows.

Although proprietary studies of audience behavior have occurred since the earliest days of television, the first published research on repeat viewing appeared in 1975 (Goodhardt, Ehrenberg, & Collins, 1975). The picture that emerged suggested that repeat viewing for all television series hovered at around 55%. In other words, of those who saw a program one day, just over half would watch the following episode either the next day or the next week, no matter when it was broadcast. This level of audience turnover occurred even though the program rating of each individual episode remained constant. Furthermore, most studies found no variation in repeat viewing by the type of series under investigation, although subsequent research reported moderately higher levels of repeat viewing for soap operas (Barwise, Ehrenberg, & Goodhardt, 1982).

Like inheritance effects, the overall phenomenon evidently results from underlying patterns of audience availability. In the case of repeat viewing, the 55% level occurs because most of the missing 45% simply aren't watching television (Barwise et al., 1982). If, as we argued in chapter 2, the causes of nonviewing are unrelated to available program content, then audience behavior that is related to nonviewing might be similarly unrelated to content. This seems to be the case with repeat viewing.

To the extent that any factor has been associated with variation in repeat viewing of series television, the most important correlate has been the ratings level of the program in question (Goodhardt et al., 1987; Sherman, 1995). The higher the average rating of a series, the higher the average level of repeat viewing. This result is yet another example of a double jeopardy effect.

Most of the early studies of repeat viewing on U.S. audiences used commercially collected television diary data to measure audience behavior. Because of standard diary placement and retrieval techniques (Webster & Lichty, 1991; Webster & Wakshlag, 1985), their use effectively constrained the type of program that could be examined to those that were stripped across several days of the week. It also meant that relatively little prime time programming could be examined. Furthermore, the use of diary data seems to have predisposed researchers to base their measures of repeat viewing on individual rather than on household patterns.

The scope of repeat viewing research expanded somewhat in the mid-1980s with the publication of Barwise's (1986) secondary analysis of Nielsen data. These data, including some based on conventional household meters, produced repeat viewing levels slightly lower than those reported earlier. By the late 1980s, however, a different and somewhat confusing picture began to emerge. Using peoplemeter data generated by the Boston test-marketing of Audits of Great Britain's (AGB) rating service, Ehrenberg and Wakshlag (1987) found repeat viewing levels on the order of 25%. Although certain characteristics of the Boston market, including atypical program scheduling, might lead one to doubt the generalizability of their results, peoplemeter data collected in Denver a year later produced similarly low levels of repeat viewing (Soong, 1988). The characteristics and results of all of these studies of repeat viewing are summarized in Table 5.1.

What remains unclear is why these changes have occurred, and what levels of repeat viewing now exist across the wide variety of program types broadcast at different times of the day. It may well be that dramatic changes in the viewing environment have diminished the loyalty of audiences to all television series. Indeed, to the extent that new technologies like cable and VCRs have reduced the size of network audiences, the application of simple double jeopardy logic would predict that lower repeat viewing levels should follow. It might also be that the nationwide scheme of peoplemeter measurement introduced by the A.C. Nielsen Company in 1987 somehow produced an artifact of lower repeat viewing. Certainly the two developments were confounded. Hence, it would seem appropriate to reevaluate national patterns of repeat viewing in the wake of those developments.

DETERMINANTS OF REPEAT VIEWING

Beyond a simple description of repeat viewing levels, however, a systematic examination of factors that contribute to variation in those levels is desirable. With the exception of double jeopardy effects, relatively little work has been done in this area. Furthermore, there is cause to question the generalizability of what has been reported, and good reason to explore other determinants of repeat viewing that have received insufficient attention.

As we argued in chapter 2, the most powerful determinants of mass audience behavior, like repeat viewing, are structural. Chief among those structural variables are patterns of audience availability and program scheduling characteristics. Operationally, that would suggest investigating: (a) variation by dayparts, which are known to be associated with patterns of availability, and (b) whether the series in question was stripped across weekdays, or broadcast once a week. Specifically, off-peak dayparts (i.e., non-prime time) are thought to serve viewers who are more regularly available (Goodhardt et al. 1987). Hence, we would expect higher levels of repeat viewing to be associated with non-prime time dayparts. Because stripped programming is identified with these dayparts, we would similarly predict higher levels of repeat viewing to be associated with that programming strategy.

Double jeopardy, at least as it has been operationalized and tested by Goodhardt et al. (1987), would further suggest that the average program rating of a television series is positively correlated with its level of repeat viewing. Despite claims for the prevalence of double jeopardy effects (e.g., Ehrenberg et al., 1990), recent research by Barnes (1990) found some exceptions to those effects in channel-rich environments. Given that, and the

TABLE 5.1
A Summary of Research on Repeat Viewing of Network Programs

Reference	Sample	Method	Program Scheduling	Unit of Analysis	Repeat Viewing %	
					Average	Range
Goodhart et al. (1975, 1987)	London Apr./May, 1971	Diaries	week-to-week;	housewives	55	45-65
	New York City Jan/Feb, 1974		stripped within the week, early fringe	housewives	53	21-70
Headen et al. (1979)	U.S. National 1972	Diaries	day-to-day, all dayparts prime	individuals	48 53	25-66
Barwise et al. (1982)	New York City	Diaries	day-to-day daytime and early fringe;	adults	53	41-66
	Los Angeles Oct., 1976		week-to-week, all dayparts and primetime	adults	46 48	21-64
Barwise (1986)	Two cable franchise areas (April, May, 1982) Nielsen NAC	Diaries	week-to-week primetime	adults and teenagers	36	
		Diaries	week-to-week primetime	household	48	
	Oct, 1983—March, 1984 Nielsen NTI Feb., 1984	Audimeter	week-to-week primetime	adults households	41 45	37-45 23-67
Ehrenberg & Wakshlag (1987)	Boston May/June, 1985	Peoplemeter	week-to-week, afternoon, evening	household adults	26 25	
Soong (1988)	Denver and Boulder May, 1986	Peoplemeter	week-to-week, different dayparts	household adults	28 24	

Adapted from Webster and Wang, 1992.

counterintuitive nature of double jeopardy, it seems appropriate to test just how robust these effects are in the context of repeat viewing.

Although all of the factors just discussed might be thought of as structuralist in nature, and hence are given a theoretical preference in our approach to explaining audience behavior, we are not in a position to specify, a priori, what will be the most powerful determinant of repeat viewing. Rather, we have elected to explore their interrelationships through the correlational analyses reported later.

Finally, the content of a television series would seem to have implications for patterns of repeat viewing. Notwithstanding the audience for soap operas, as recently as 1987, Goodhardt et al. reported "there is virtually no systematic variation by programme type or content. Repeat-viewing of a serial with a continuing story-line is generally not higher than that for a regular film slot with radically different showings each week" (p. 114). Given the importance of content-related preferences in many social scientific investigations of exposure or readership, this is a remarkable finding. Certainly intuition would suggest that a continuing storyline would draw curious viewers from one episode to the next, thereby producing higher levels of repeat viewing. In fact, this expectation would seem most consistent with theories touting individual level features of the audience as the principle determinants of behavior (see chapter 2).

To test this hypothesis, we operationalized program type as continuing versus noncontinuing storyline. Although it might be argued that nightly news or situation comedies have continuing storylines, we opted for a stricter definition. Specifically, only programs identified as "daytime drama" (i.e., soap operas) by the Nielsen Television Index were coded as continuing. Other candidates for such coding, like "prime time soaps" (e.g., *Dallas*, *Falcon Crest*), were scheduled with insufficient frequency to allow analysis. Adopting this rather conservative approach to coding, we believed, offered the best opportunity for program-type effects to emerge.

METHOD: CUMULATIVE MEASURES
FROM AGGREGATE DATA

This research is a cumulative analysis based on A.C. Nielsen peoplemeter data collected over a 4-week period ending October 23, 1988, as reported in the NTI's *Program Cumulative Audiences* (Nielsen Television Index, 1988). The Nielsen sample included over 4,000 households, of which 3,222 qualified for inclusion by providing usable data on at least 3 of the 4 weeks covered by the report.

The *Program Cumulative Audiences* report lists all broadcast network programs that aired during the period, the weeks in which they were broadcast, the average household rating per telecast, the total number of times the program aired (ranging from 1 to 20), and the percent of TV households that saw 1, 2, and 3, or up to as many as 20 telecasts during the survey period. The same sort of report, only based on household meters, was used by Barwise (1986) to assess repeat viewing. Unfortunately, these reports do not contain a program-by-program summary of repeat viewing that is directly comparable with published research on the subject (i.e., the usual percentages described in Table 5.1). However, Barwise devised a method for translating aggregate data on the distribution of households watching one or more telecasts into the summary statistic commonly reported in the academic literature.

Essentially, Barwise (1986) assumed that the percentage of households watching some number of telecasts is evenly distributed over the number of times in the four-week period that the program is actually aired. He explained, taking the example of a series broadcast three times:

> For every thousand homes, suppose 210 saw exactly one episode, 90 saw two episodes, and 50 saw all three. Each episode would be seen by one-third of the 210 (i.e., 70) plus two-thirds of the 90 (i.e., 60) plus all of the 50 (i.e., 50). This equals 180 homes out of 1,000, equivalent to a rating of 18 points. (p. 10)

Once an assumption about the distribution of viewing is made, it is relatively easy to impute a level of repeat viewing. In the case just stated, none of 70 homes repeat viewed, 30 of 60 repeat viewed, and 50 of 50 did as well. Therefore, of the 180 homes watching a typical episode, an average of 80 (i.e., 0 + 30 + 50) were repeat viewers, resulting in a repeat viewing rate of 44% (i.e., 80/180).

By applying this method, we were able to estimate the average percent of repeat viewing for each program in the report. This measure is essentially the same as those reported in Table 5.1. It should be noted, however, that using the Barwise (1986) method to derive measures from aggregate data may be more prone to error than those based on individual level data because the distribution of repeat viewing is assumed rather than actually observed.

Network programs were the unit of analysis. To qualify for inclusion, each program had to have been broadcast at least twice during the four-week period. Shows that aired only once obviously presented no data on repeat viewing. This requirement eliminated many programs, including special reports, Summer Olympic coverage during the first week, and World Series coverage during the fourth week. A total of 145 regular network programs were thus identified for the analysis.

Each program was described on a number of variables. The dependent variable was the average percent of repeat viewing as determined by the Barwise (1986) translation. Initially, there were four independent variables: (a) the average household rating per telecast, as reported by Nielsen, which

TABLE 5.2
Repeat Viewing Levels by Dayparts, Ratings, and Telecasts Per Week

Range of Program Ratings	Number of Programs	Telecasts Per Week	Average Rating	Average Repeat Viewing
Prime Time (7:30–11:00 p.m.)				
20.0–24.9%	N = 2	1	22.0	47.4
15.0–19.9%	N = 9	1	17.5	42.3
10.0–14.9%	N = 15	1	12.4	32.0
Less than 9.9%	N = 10	1	8.1	26.4
All Cases .	N = 36	1	15.0	32.7
Weekday Daytime (10:00 a.m.–5:00 p.m.)				
6.0–7.9%	N = 4	5	6.5	62.1
4.0–5.9%	N = 8	5	4.9	57.5
Less than 4.0%	N = 12	5	2.8	51.7
All Cases	N = 24	5	4.2	55.5
Weekend Daytime (8:00 a.m.–5:00 p.m.)				
10.0–14.9%	N = 4	1	11.4	33.3
6.0–9.9%	N = 1	1	9.1	26.5
4.0–5.9%	N = 20	1	4.9	23.6
Less than 4.0%	N = 24	1	2.6	21.2
All Cases	N = 49	1	3.7	23.3
Weekday Morning (6:00–10:00 a.m.)				
All cases	N =10	5	3.2	50.1
Weekday Evening Network News				
All cases	N = 3	5	9.8	55.1
Weekday Late Night				
All cases	N = 8	5	3.1	44.2

we hypothesized was positively correlated with repeat viewing, (b) the daypart in which the program appeared, which was coded as a series of dummy variables, with the prediction that repeat viewing would be highest in non-prime time dayparts, (c) the frequency of telecast, nominally coded 5 for a program airing five days a week, and 1 for a program airing once a week, with the prediction that stripped programming would enjoy higher rates of repeat viewing, and (d) the program type, coded 1 if it had a continuing story line, and 0 if it did not, hypothesizing that the former would be associated with higher repeat viewing. These variables were first used to provide a simple descriptive summary of repeat viewing levels, and then employed in the correlational analyses reported in results.

Table 5.2 reports average levels of repeat viewing by selected dayparts and the ratings level of the programs within dayparts. Programs falling outside these categories were too few in number to offer stable reporting categories, hence the table is based on a subset of the full sample of programs. Three things are worthy of note. First, there is considerable variation in the level of repeat viewing across these program categories:

averages range from the low 20s to the low 60s. Second, there does not appear to be a simple double jeopardy effect operating across all program categories. Indeed, the highest levels of repeat viewing are associated with daytime programs that have considerably lower ratings than prime-time programming. There is, however, a substantial double jeopardy effect within dayparts. Third, as might be expected, there is a complete confounding of daypart with the number of times a program is telecast. Daytime programs are stripped 5 days a week whereas prime time programs are aired once a week. Because of this confounding, the correlational analyses that follow considered only one scheduling variable with a dummy coding of either 1 *(stripped across 5 days a week)*, or 0 *(broadcast once a week)*.

A more precise measure of relationships across the full sample of programs can be seen in Table 5.3, which is a correlation matrix of the repeat viewing variable and three independent variables. This table confirms what was suggested in Table 5.2. There is an insignificant correlation between the average ratings of a television series and repeat viewing of that series $(r = .100)$. There is, however, a powerful relationship $(r = .789)$ between how a program is scheduled and repeat viewing levels. There is also a significant relationship between repeat viewing and program type $(r = .498)$. On the face of it, a continuing storyline is associated with higher levels of repeat viewing. The interpretation of this relationship is complicated by an inter-correlation with scheduling $(r = .441)$, as should be expected because all programs with a continuing storyline were daytime dramas. A clearer picture of how these variables act in concert can be seen in Table 5.4.

Table 5.4 presents the results of an OLS multiple regression procedure in which the three predictor variables shown in Table 5.3 were entered simultaneously. As would be expected from the correlation matrix, the most powerful determinant of repeat viewing is the program scheduling variable. With daypart differences accounted for by scheduling, ratings prove to be a highly significant determinant of repeat viewing. Program type also adds significantly to the explanatory power of this three variable

TABLE 5.3
Correlation Matrix of Repeat Viewing

Variables	2	3	4
1. Repeat Viewing Rate	.789*	.100	.498*
2. Scheduling		-.372*	.441*
3. Rating			-.083
4. Program Type			

*Two tailed test of significance $p < .001$

TABLE 5.4
Determinants of Repeat Viewing

Variables	Beta Coefficients	T Value
Scheduling	.904	21.922*
Rating	.448	12.046*
Program Type	.137	3.553*

*T Value significant $p < .001$

model. Overall, the model is highly significant ($F = 236$; df 3,141; $p < .0001$) and explains over 80% of the variance ($R^2 = .83$) in the dependent variable.

DISCUSSION: SCHEDULING AND CONTENT

The notion that repeat viewing levels for most television series hover at around 55% no longer squares with the facts. Some series attain that level of repeat viewing but most do not. However, variation in repeat viewing levels is quite predictable as long as we consider the scheduling characteristics of programs and, to a lesser extent, their content.

The most important correlates of repeat viewing are what we have referred to as structural factors. Of these, the scheduling factor was the most powerful determinant of repeat viewing. In this study, that variable was a combination of two confounded factors: daypart, which was a surrogate for availability, and stripped versus nonstripped programming. Although we are inclined to think that exogenous factors produce a greater regularity of viewing during off-peak dayparts, and hence higher levels of repeat viewing, we cannot discount the impact of programming. In fact, it is likely that the two combine to encourage a certain regularity of habit in viewing during these dayparts. Future research should attempt to disentangle these factors, perhaps by examining repeat viewing of prime-time miniseries, or other instances where stripped and nonstripped programming compete in the same daypart.

Contrary to earlier research, we found simple, across-the-board double jeopardy effects to be nonexistent. Knowing the average rating of a program, by itself, provides almost no basis for predicting a corresponding level of repeat viewing. However, when ratings level is combined with scheduling information about the program, it becomes a useful predictor. These two structural factors should be the key elements in attempts to model the reach and frequency of exposure to television programs and advertising campaigns.

Program type, at least as we operationalized it, was also a significant predictor of repeat viewing. As reported elsewhere in the literature, soap operas are associated with higher levels of repeat viewing. Our results, however, raise the possibility that much of this effect may be attributable to the daypart in which they are broadcast. Again, further work, featuring a larger and more diverse sample of series with continuing storylines, should be undertaken to clarify the role of program type in repeat viewing (e.g., Sherman, 1995).

In addition to further research on the predictor variables examined here, at least three other factors should be examined in an effort to produce a more complete understanding of repeat viewing. All are suggested in the model of audience behavior presented in chapter 2. They are, in what we believe is their order of importance: (a) the number of available channels, (b) group-viewing configurations, and (c) VCR ownership.

It is well-established that audiences in channel-rich environments become relatively fragmented, producing lower average program ratings (Barnes, 1990; Webster, 1989b). The double jeopardy phenomenon predicts that, all things being equal, such environments would feature lower repeat viewing rates as well. Although the existence of channel repertoires (Heeter & Greenberg, 1988) may impose a kind of ceiling effect on multichannel environments, it would nonetheless be interesting to compare repeat viewing across the number of channels available.

At the level of individual audience factors, the nature of group viewing configurations over time is likely to affect repeat viewing. For example, Webster and Wakshlag (1982) demonstrated that when program decision-making groups remained constant over time, households demonstrated significantly greater evidence of program-type loyalty. Similarly, it is plausible that if the same person or persons are in charge of program selection when the episodes of a series are broadcast, then greater constancy of choice (i.e., repeat viewing) will result. Indeed, constancy of decision making may be associated with dayparts, and responsible in some measure for the scheduling effects reported here.

In theory, VCR ownership could be a potent determinant of repeat viewing because it allows an individual to counteract the structural factors that seem to be responsible for patterns of repeat viewing. If neither audience availability, nor program schedules constrain program choice, then repeat viewing might be fundamentally different. As a practical matter, however, evidence suggests that people with VCRs tape relatively few programs, and much of what is taped is never watched (Levy & Fink, 1984).

As we noted at the outset, repeat viewing is an elemental form of mass behavior that, when aggregated over many occasions, reveals a good deal about cumulative patterns of exposure. For instance, extending the phenomenon of repeat viewing across an entire series can produce models of exposure that accurately predict how many people will see a specific number of episodes (Barwise, 1986). As it turns out, only a tiny portion of the audience sees a majority of the episodes in any given series (Goodhardt et al., 1987). Such data are of obvious relevance to media planners intent on estimating media reach and frequency. But they have broader implications for how to use television in instruction and information campaigns. To the extent that patterns of exposure, like repeat viewing, delimit the effects of television, they should be of concern to social scientists and policymakers alike.

Chapter 6

Television News
Audiences

Perhaps no television genre is of broader interest than the news. It commands the attention of social scientists and critics of popular culture who believe it exerts a powerful influence on society. It has long been a concern of policymakers intent on promoting the public interest. It is an important determinant of a network's prestige, as well as a significant source of revenues. On the local level, many of these concerns are magnified. The local news helps to galvanize social action and promote a sense of community. It defines a station's image in the market and serves as a profit center that need not be shared with other networks or syndicators. In all of these matters, the size of the news audience is of critical importance.

PERSPECTIVES ON THE NEWS AUDIENCE

There are different ways to explain exposure to news programming. As we suggested in chapter 2, theories of audience behavior can be broadly categorized into one of two sorts, distinguished primarily by their level of analysis. The first approach emphasizes the primacy of individual viewer characteristics in determining program choices. The second focuses on structural characteristics as the key determinants of audience formation. Although there have been efforts to both contrast and integrate these perspectives (McQuail & Gurevitch, 1974; Webster & Wakshlag, 1983; Weibull, 1985), a marriage of the two has been difficult to arrange.

The first perspective is best represented by the long tradition of research in selective exposure (e.g., Zillmann & Bryant, 1985). It is also evident in much "uses and gratifications" research, which explicitly claims an interest in "differential patterns of media exposure" (Katz, Blumler, & Gurevitch, 1974, p. 20). Under either approach, exposure to television is thought to be determined by an individual's cognitive and/or affective condition. Studies that have focused specifically on the audience for broadcast news have, therefore, concentrated on viewer preferences, and sought gratifications as determinants of news attendance (e.g., Babrow & Swanson, 1988; Levy, 1978; Palmgreen, Wenner, & Rayburn, 1981; Rubin & Perse, 1987; Wulfemeyer, 1983). Such work often studies individual behaviors in uniform media environments where structural factors do not vary. Hence, the impact of media structures (e.g., program scheduling, market characteristics, etc.) is often left unexamined.

Illustrative of the second perspective are research and theory in marketing and economics. Here, explanations of exposure tend to focus on structural factors like audience availabilities and the juxtaposition of programs within and across channels. We reviewed many studies of this type in the preceding chapters. In the case of news watching, the audience is typically conceived of as a mass that is shaped by various market characteristics (e.g., Baldwin, Barnett, & Bates, 1992; Boemer, 1987; Wakshlag, Agostino, Terry, Driscoll, & Ramsey, 1983; Webster, 1984; Webster & Newton, 1988). Under this perspective, researchers will often analyze aggregated rather than individual level data. The research also tends to eschew the motivational states of viewers, in part because it is not theoretically central to the investigation, and also because such work often involves a secondary analysis of ratings data that are themselves devoid of those viewer traits.

This study is grounded in the latter tradition of audience research and focuses directly on the impact that structural factors have on the size of the local news audience. It is based, in part, on a study by Webster and Newton (1988). In keeping with the spirit of this book, we concentrate on understanding news attendance as a matter of mass audience behavior.

DETERMINANTS OF AUDIENCE FORMATION

There are several structural features of both the audience and the media that are likely to affect the news audience. For convenience, these can be organized into two categories: (a) long-term market characteristics that are largely beyond the control of broadcasters, and (b) relatively transitory program scheduling characteristics that are within the control of local stations. The rationale for including specific variables in one or the other category is discussed in the following paragraphs.

Among the long-term factors, one of the most powerful determinants of who sees a given television program is audience availability. Total audience size varies predictably by hour of the day, day of the week, and week of the year. This variation seems almost completely independent of program offerings, hence television programmers have long considered total audience size a given, and attempted only to increase their share of the pie. In this context, the available audience is conceptualized as a given market characteristic. Consistent with earlier arguments (e.g., Gensch & Shaman, 1980; Webster & Lichty, 1991), it is operationalized as the total audience using the medium at a point in time. Another market condition that is likely to affect exposure to a program is the number of channels available to viewers. As competition in the market increases, either through the introduction of independent commercial stations or cable, we would expect greater audience fragmentation and, on average, lower ratings for any one channel (Baldwin et al., 1992; Owen & Wildman, 1992; Webster, 1984, 1986). Finally, stations may themselves have more or less desirable channel assignments. It is widely believed, for example, that broadcasting on a UHF frequency "handicaps" a station (Webster, 1983).

Among the more transitory factors that can affect the audience for news is how programs are scheduled. In chapter 4, we reviewed a considerable body of literature that documented the pervasiveness of inheritance effects. That research, not to mention the conventional wisdom of programmers, suggests there is a considerable benefit to be gained by scheduling the news after a highly rated program. The more people who watch the first program, the more viewers there are to be led into the news. Furthermore, the inheritance effect is thought to be especially strong when the adjacent programs are a station's local and network news (Wakshlag et al., 1983). In contrast to such within-channel effects, are the counterprogramming strategies employed by competing stations. These too may be especially pronounced during the broadcast of local news. As Haldi (1981) noted, "if one cannot win with better news, then one can split the viewing audience by scheduling entertainment programs against the news. . . [because] about a third of the audience does not want to watch the news to begin with" (p. 99).

METHOD: GROSS MEASURES OF AUDIENCE SIZE

Unlike the cumulative analyses presented in chapters 4 and 5, this research relies on gross measures of audience size. It is a correlational study that explores how the various independent variables, suggested in the review, affect local news ratings. Data were obtained from the February 1986 Nielsen Station Index report, including all designated marketing areas (DMAs) in the United States. From this universe, a random sample of 40 markets was drawn. Because market structure (e.g., number of stations, etc.) was highly relevant to the investigation, the sample was stratified with respect to market rank. Specifically, ten markets were drawn from DMAs ranked 1–50, 51–100, 101–150, and 151+, respectively. In these markets, each network affiliate's early evening local news program became a unit of analysis. Because not all markets have three network affiliates with measurable local news audiences, this procedure produced a sample of 103 usable cases.

In all instances, the ratings data used were the 4-week quarter hour average for all persons 2+. In a few markets, a station's early evening local news appeared in more than one distinct program length segment. For consistency, local news ratings were defined by audience size during the first quarter hour of each station's early evening news programming, even though additional segments occasionally followed. All other program ratings were based on the first quarter hour of the program, with the exception of lead-in ratings. The rating of any lead-in program was based on audience size during its last quarter hour, even if the lead-in program was news (e.g., local news defined as lead-in to network news).

The analysis was operationalized in such a way as to create one dependent variable (local news rating) and nine independent variables. Following the distinction made in the review, variables were grouped as long-term market characteristics or short-term programming characteristics. Market variables were: (a) the available audience size, defined as the number of *persons using television* (PUT) at the time the local news was broadcast, (b) the number of commercial independents in the market, (c) percentage of cable penetration in the DMA, and (d) the station's channel assignment, coded either UHF = 1 or VHF = 0. Our expectation was to find a positive correlation between PUT level and ratings, and negative correlations with the other three predictors.

Programming variables were: (a) the rating of the program leading into the local news, (b) the rating of the network news program, (c) the number of local news programs being counterprogrammed, (d) the number of network news programs being counterprogrammed, and (e) the number of entertainment programs being counterprogrammed. Our expectation was to find a positive correlation between local news ratings and both lead-in and network news ratings, and negative correlations with the other predictor variables.

To explore the relationships among these ten variables, market and programming factors were, initially, treated separately. Correlation matrices for each category were generated. To assess the combined effect of these independent variables on local news, a stepwise multiple regression was performed in which all variables were allowed to enter the equation. Inspection of the skew and kurtosis of all variables indicated that deviations from normality were not sufficient to warrant data transformations.

Table 6.1 presents the correlation matrix of local news ratings and market characteristics. As expected, there was a significant positive relationship between local news ratings and the size of the available audience (i.e., PUT). There was also the expected negative correlations between news audiences, number of commercial independents in the market, and channel assignment. Contrary to expectations, the relationship between cable penetration and ratings was positive, although insignificant. There was a strong inverse relationship between cable penetration and the number of independents in the market, suggesting that cable penetration might be inversely related to market size. This may have confounded the impact of cable on local news because large market stations tend to start their local news programming earlier when audience levels are relatively low.

Table 6.2 presents the correlation matrix of programming variables. There were highly significant relationships between local news ratings, lead-in ratings, and network news ratings, all positive as predicted. Also as expected, the number of entertainment programs scheduled opposite the local news diminished ratings. Curiously, there was a significant positive relationship between local news ratings and the number of network news programs on opposite channels, suggesting that such a programming strategy is disadvantageous from the network's standpoint.

Clearly, there are very powerful relationships among lead-in ratings, network ratings, and local news ratings. In fact, in 25 of the 103 cases examined here, network news led into local news confounding these factors. To untangle these cases, separate analyses were performed. When network news led into local news, the overall correlation was .58 ($p < .01$). However, when non-news programming led into local news ($n = 78$) the correlation was .71 ($p < .001$), and when local news led into network news

TABLE 6.1
Correlation Matrix of Market Characteristics

Variables	2	3	4	5
1. Local News Rating	-.21*	.17	-.25*	.49**
2. Channel Assignment		.10	-.13	-.10
3. Cable Penetration			-.50**	.29**
4. Number of Independents				-.37**
5. Persons Using Television (PUT)				

*Pearson product-moment correlation significant $p < .05$. **Pearson product-moment correlation significant $p < .01$.

TABLE 6.2
Correlation Matrix of Programming Characteristics

Variables	2	3	4	5	6
1. Local News Rating	.75**	.82**	.03	.25**	-.29**
2. Lead-in Rating		.62**	-.14	.15	-.27**
3. Network News Rating			.01	.09	-.17
4. Number of Local News Counter-programmed				-.05	-.27**
5. Number of Network News Counter-programmed					-.19*
6. Number of Entertainment Counter-programmed					

*Pearson product-moment correlation significant $p < .05$. **Pearson product-moment correlation significant $p < .01$.

TABLE 6.3
Determinants of Local News Ratings

| | Beta Weights | | |
Independent Variables	Step 1	Step 2	Step 3
Network News Ratings	.82	.57	.55
Lead-in Rating		.39	.32
PUT Level			.25
R^2	.67	.76	.81
Overall F	205.46*	163.77*	151.74*
df	1,101	2,100	3,99

*Overall F significant $p < .01$.

($n = 78$) the correlation was a remarkable .96 ($p < .001$). These results suggest that the overall relationship between network news and local news was determined more by the strength of the local news than vice versa.

Market and programming factors are, of course, not independent of one another. To assess the combined effect of these variables on local news ratings, a stepwise regression was performed. Table 6.3 presents the results of the analysis.

One market variable, PUT level, and two programming variables, lead-in and network news ratings, combined to explain more than 80% of the variance in local news ratings. No other variables added significant explanatory power to the equation.

DISCUSSION: MEDIA STRUCTURE
AND AUDIENCE FORMATION

Structural factors have a tremendous impact on the size of program audiences. In the case of news viewing, the results highlight the importance of within-channel scheduling effects in determining who sees a local news program. None of these relationships is more intriguing than the close link between the network news audience and the local news audience. Although these data do not allow us to measure the amount of audience flow from one program to the next, the high correlations provide considerable circumstantial evidence that this is precisely what happens. In a similar vein, Cooper (1993) demonstrated that inheritance effects are a crucial determinant of syndicated program ratings. Once again, the results underscore the difficulty of understanding exposure without reference to the structure of available programming.

Indeed, media structures are likely to become even more important in the years to come. As we argue in chapter 7, audience theory has grown up in a world where a small number of channels have been universally available. But that world is rapidly giving way to one in which a large number of channels are differentially available to viewers. As this happens, examining variation in program audiences across market conditions will be essential to understanding why some programs enjoy a large audience and others do not. Unless people watch a genre in large numbers, most of the economic and social concerns we described at the outset are moot.

In a larger sense, the results should draw the attention of scholars to the significance of structural factors in audience behavior. This is not to say that an individual's desires and expectations are unimportant causes of media exposure. Surely, some fundamental needs provide the impetus for seeking out news and entertainment. But how those needs ultimately find expression is powerfully affected by the media environment and merits fuller consideration. For instance, we have seen in this and many other studies how the interplay of audience availability and program schedules affect exposure to program content. Yet, as Elliott (1974) noted some years ago "availability in any sense rarely finds a place in uses and gratifications research" (p. 259). That is still largely true today. If we are to advance our knowledge of patterns of exposure to media, then the strengths of each of the perspectives we outlined must be more adequately exploited.

One factor that has divided these approaches, is the level of analysis at which each tends to operate. Typical of its kind, this study examined aggregate audience data (i.e., the ratings). However, having demonstrated strong relationships to media structures at this level of analysis, it might be useful to develop analogous variables for research at the individual level of analysis. For example, in addition to asking people about their expectations of a medium or assessing their mood states, we might also ask when they are physically available to use the medium and what channels they can receive on their sets. To explain an individual's exposure to a particular program, we should consider not only the gratifications they seek, but the kind of alternatives they have and what programs they have watched beforehand.

There are relatively few research studies that consider individual motivations and structural factors simultaneously. McDonald and Reese (1987) provided one example of how such an approach could be applied to news audiences. Likewise, Ferguson and Perse (1993) considered the impact of gratificationist and structural factors on total channel repertoires (TCR). They concluded, "Overall audience behavior can be explained well without considering individual audience characteristics. Our findings show in a powerful way that TCR is a function of audience availability as it interacts with media structure" (p. 42).

Future research should extend this type of inquiry by deliberately introducing structural variations into their design. We suspect that research will
confirm the importance of structural factors in explaining audience behavior. In any event, knowing the power of these variables to predict an
individual's exposure to either the medium or specific content would be
illuminating.

Chapter 7

The New Media
Environment

What is the future of the mass audience in an age of technological abundance? Will an explosion of new media reduce what we have learned in the preceding pages to a quaint historical footnote? There has been no shortage of scholarship addressing such questions (e.g., Becker & Schoenbach, 1989; Dizard, 1994; Dobrow, 1990; Neuman, 1991; Salvaggio & Bryant, 1989). What is in short supply is a consensus about what the future holds. Some are inclined to think that great changes are afoot:

> Consumers are now armed with new viewing devices like VCRs, remote control tuners, and addressable converters, which free them from the carefully planned programming schedules of the network architects and permit them access to an astounding number and variety of program choices. Old programming theories based on a scarce number of offerings and a passive, inert audience no longer seem meaningful and cannot be accepted as the standard catechism in this space-age jungle of programming abundance. (Litman & Kohl, 1992, p. 391)

Other students of the audience offer a more conservative prognosis. As Barwise and Ehrenberg (1988) stated, "Thirty years from now, we believe, television will still be a mass medium with largely unsegmented audiences watching varied programs for many hours and mostly at a low level of involvement" (p. 121).

Forecasting is always a perilous business. A decade ago, Webster (1986) proposed a framework for understanding how the new media environment would affect audience behavior. Although it was developed to address the future of the television audience, it seems sufficiently robust to structure a more general discussion of mass audiences. Hence, we use it as the basis for our foray into the future.

CHANGES IN THE MEDIA ENVIRONMENT

In the latter part of the 20th century, we have seen significant changes in the nature of mass media. Magazine titles have proliferated as they target ever more discrete market segments. Radio has adopted a similar strategy of offering specialized formats. Major newspapers have begun to "zone" advertising and editorial content as a step along the way to a more tailored product. Television, our vast cultural forum, has undergone the most dramatic changes of all. The number of channels entering the home has mushroomed, VCRs have become almost as commonplace as television sets, and *broadband computer networks* have grown, offering the tantalizing prospect of video on demand. Because one of the recurring themes of this book is that media structures have a powerful impact on audience behavior, a review of changes in the media environment seems an appropriate place to begin.

Our approach is to highlight critical differences in what we term "old" and "new" media environments. The *old media environment* is characterized by limited channels of communication that deliver content on a fixed timetable of the media's choosing. The *new media environment* is distinguished by unlimited channels of communication offering content on a timetable of the individual's choosing. We compare old and new on three attributes that seem particularly relevant to audience behavior: diversity of content, correlation of content with channels, and availability. As we demonstrate, each environment is the polar opposite of the other along these dimensions.

We should emphasize that these portrayals of old and new are meant to be abstractions rather than accurate descriptions of any media systems that ever were or will be. They are theoretical anchors that help us to locate where we have been and where we might be heading, and they allow us to draw out the implications of different interpretations of media. They are important for what they portend about audience formation, and for the ways that they illuminate how social theory may be wedded to a particular understanding of media structure.

CHARACTERISTICS OF OLD MEDIA

Media Content Is Uniform

One of the more prevalent characterizations of the old media system is that it offers audiences an undifferentiated menu from which to choose. From this perspective, whatever variation seems to exist is superficial and of no account. Instead, all media cater to socially prevalent values and paint a uniform, if distorted, picture of social reality.

The most extreme manifestation of this view occurs in the work of critical theorists. Karl Marx and his intellectual heirs have argued that, in capitalist societies, the media are owned by a class intent on promoting certain ideas and extinguishing others. As Marx and Engels (1976) stated over a century ago, "the ideas of the ruling class are, in every age, the ruling ideas" (p. 70).

Viewed in this light, mass media are agents of class domination, facilitating hegemony and promoting false consciousness.

Even those inclined to take a more "liberal–pluralist" view of society, however, reach a similar conclusion when considering old media. Once again, the culprit is capitalism. Commercial mass media are generally interested in attracting as many readers or viewers as possible. Given this overriding concern with maximizing audiences, the media are loath to present anything that might offend or alienate even a modest portion of the public. Rather, they resort to formulas and themes that can easily be accepted by the broadest possible audience.

Such characterizations of the media are hardly new. Klapper (1960) noted that the argument was popular as early as the late 1940s, and he concluded that, despite some exceptions, "the economic character of commercial media in a free enterprise society is such that they appear destined forever to play to, and thus reinforce, socially prevalent attitudes" (p. 42). In fact, it seems an apt description of the mass circulation magazines and broadcast networks that dominated American media in the 1950s. Nor has this line of reasoning lost much of its appeal in the intervening years. Many contemporary analysts from both ends of the political spectrum have portrayed the media as inexorably committed to the production of standardized content (e.g., Bagdikian, 1992; Gerbner & Gross, 1976; Murdock & Golding, 1977; Neuman, 1982; Noelle-Neuman, 1973).

Content Is Uncorrelated With Channels

If all content is the same, it is impossible for one channel of communication to offer something that is genuinely different from the competition. In the case of commercial television, this has meant no significant difference in what a viewer could see on ABC, CBS, or NBC. Indeed, this condition is consistent with the predictions of formal models of network behavior. Owen, Beebe, and Manning (1974) noted such duplication of program content

> occurs because there is a tendency for a decentralized system of broadcasting, with limited channel capacity, to produce rivalry for large blocks of the audience with programs that are, if not identical, at least close substitutes. There is a tendency, in our case, for the three networks to produce the same kind of programming. (p. 101)

As a practical matter, characterizing television in this way has allowed theorists to treat it as a single, undifferentiated medium. Nowhere is this strategy more evident than in the work of Gerbner and Gross (1976) who argued that "the 'world' of television is an organic system of stories and images" (p. 180). Only the absolute rate of exposure to television is needed or, for that matter, appropriate as an independent variable. Even among researchers who might not adopt *cultivation analysis* as a theoretical framework, television, as a cause of social or psychological effects, has often been "considered globally" (Cook, Kendzierski, & Thomas, 1983, p. 164).

Content Is Universally Available

If content is the same from one channel of communication to the next, then contact with any channel brings with it the entire universe of content. As we noted in chapter 1, newspapers covered most of the population before the end of the 19th century. By the early 20th century, broadcasting surpassed even the reach of print media. Throughout the United States and much of the industrialized world, mass media, and all they have to offer, are universally available. Television, in particular, "penetrates every home in the land" (Gerbner & Gross, 1976, p. 175).

Represented as such a uniform, inescapable presence, the only relevant feature of audience behavior would seem to be how much of the medium is actually consumed. Descriptions of television's omnipresent quality, therefore, are quite often accompanied by statistical summaries of the enormous amount of time people spend watching television (e.g., Gerbner, Gross, Morgan, & Signorielli, 1986; Neuman, 1982). Once it is documented that exposure occurs in massive doses, many social theorists have been inclined to regard further questions of audience behavior as trivial.

Right or wrong, such characterizations of the medium and its audience have had significant implications for theorizing about the medium's social impact. Indeed, the assertion that media present a homogeneous system of messages, so pervasive and uniform as to override mechanisms of selectivity, is at the heart of the arguments urging a return to the concept of powerful media effects (e.g., Noelle-Neumann, 1973; Signorielli, 1986). We consider this issue more completely in chapter 8.

CHARACTERISTICS OF NEW MEDIA

Content Is Diverse

One of the most widely touted benefits of new media is their ability to promote diversity. The veracity of that claim depends, in large part, on how one defines diversity (Kubey, Shifflet, Weerakkody, & Ukeiley, 1995; McQuail, 1992). To some, diversity means little more than increasing the number of choices available to the audience. Certainly technologies like VCRs, cable, and broadband computer networks have the practical effect of increasing what a person can see or read. To the harshest critics, however, diversity means much more than sheer number of options. It is linked more to the qualitative content of those options. They argue that genuine diversity is impossible as long as the media are controlled by a small group of corporations. Although we are not particularly sympathetic to the latter viewpoint, diversity is admittedly an elusive thing. Our position is simply that diversity can be imagined as a destination and that, in theory, it is more characteristic of new than old media environments.

Despite the arguments reviewed earlier, a good case can be made that the competitive character of mass media does not inevitably lead to the production of uniform program content catering only to the broadest possible audience (Hirsch, 1982). To be sure, the owners of media seek to maximize long-run profits, but the strategies for achieving that end may change as the competitive environment changes. In the case of the major broadcast networks, the limited number of channels predetermined the strategy of audience maximization just outlined. Economic models of audience behavior, however, suggest that this is not a necessary result if the number of channels, and hence competing services, is unconstrained (e.g., Owen & Wildman, 1992; Waterman, 1992).

Under an assumption of unlimited channels, alternative profit-making strategies emerge. Specifically, it may now be desirable, and profitable, to produce minority interest content for relatively small segments of the audience, particularly if those segments have characteristics appealing to advertisers (Barnes, 1990). In the process of doing so, it is possible, perhaps even necessary, to offend large portions of the public. This seems to have happened with some radio programming in highly competitive markets. Furthermore, if one considers technologies where the intensity of audience preferences can be reflected in direct payments, it may be feasible to produce genuine esoterica for very small segments of the audience, as long as they are willing and able to pay for it.

The factor that opens the door for such possibilities is an increase in the channel capacity of the delivery system. Virtually all new media contribute to that general expansion. In the United States, the most important of these has been cable television. As recently as 1981, the average household received nine television signals. By 1993, with the inclusion of cable, the average home received some 40 channels (Nielsen Media Research, 1993). As systems upgrade their technology and other would-be providers of broadband service enter the market, that number should continue to rise.

The availability of increased channel capacity does not, of course guarantee that diverse programming will be produced. Nevertheless, given the relative youth of most new media, relatively heterogeneous content has begun to appear. Perhaps the most significant is programming that caters to ethnic and racial minorities. Wilson and Gutierrez (1985) went so far as to argue that the growth of minority media foretells the end of mass communication. Additionally, there is increased variety in news and information, sports, children's programming, religious media, and, of course, entertainment. None of this differentiation would have been feasible under the old delivery system. How far it will go depends on a complex interplay of factors including the attractiveness of audience subsets to advertisers (Owen & Wildman, 1992), the nature of audience preferences and habits (Barwise & Ehrenberg, 1988; Neuman, 1991), the feasibility of direct payment for content (Poltrack, 1983; Wildman & Owen, 1985), the cost of producing various program forms (Barwise & Ehrenberg, 1988; Waterman, 1992), and a variety of structural and regulatory matters (Neuman, 1991; Wildman & Owen, 1985).

Content Is Correlated With Channels

As diversity increases, new questions arise about how that content is to be organized and delivered. Will publishers and programmers continue to offer channels of content indistinguishable from their competitors, or will some channels position themselves as purveyors of relatively specialized material designed for subsets of the mass audience? The answer is almost certainly the latter.

There is evidence that magazines and radio have already moved to narrowly appealing content formats. But will television, the most massified of all media, become a panoply of narrowcast channels? We have seen theories of social psychology and economic models of program choice that assume audiences with relatively consistent differential preference for program types (Webster & Wakshlag, 1983). We also know that television programmers try to exploit inheritance effects by scheduling a succession of programs with similar appeal. Both the theory and practice of managing audience flow, then, suggest organizing content by types into channels (Rust & Donthu, 1988). This, in combination with organizational factors that make it more efficient for a firm to specialize in acquisition and production of one type of programming (e.g., news, sports, etc.), should promote a correlation between channels and content.

A brief survey of how the new media have begun to organize and market themselves confirms this expectation. The Cabletelevision Advertising Bureau (1995) has reported that there are 50 video services or networks being distributed to cable systems via satellite. These include services specializing in the arts, news, sports, movies, weather, science, public affairs, financial and business information, country music, rock music, Spanish-language programming, Christian programming, Black programming, family programming, women's programming, children's programming, and adult programming.

Not all cable networks, of course, are designed to offer content of one type. A few channels have opted for a strategy that mimics the broadcast networks, and even some of the specialized services find it advantageous to maintain a degree of variation in their programming. It seems to us that a mixture of channels, some with broad appeal and many with narrow appeal, will characterize television for the foreseeable future.

But cable is not the only technology that creates a world of relatively specialized content delivered through dedicated channels. If we conceptualize a VCR as a channel that is programmed by its owner, it is entirely consistent with this characterization of new media. Levy and Fink (1984), for example, reported that video recorder users tend to specialize in a type of content. Similarly, Dobrow (1989) found that members of different subcultures used the VCR to watch ethnic programming that is otherwise unavailable to them. Assuming that the user has access to a relatively diverse program library, the content, and consequent range of diversity, of the VCR channel will be of a type defined by the viewer's preference.

Furthermore, as the media environment becomes more numerically diverse, it is likely that the audience will have to find ways to sort through the many choices confronting them. These ways would include preprogramming television sets to allow channels with acceptable content through while screening out others. Radio is already on the verge of offering digital broadcasts that will identify the format of the station, enabling listeners to automatically select only those types of predetermined programming that they expect to find interesting. Broadband service providers are experimenting with computerized editors that would sort through wire services to produce an *electronic newspaper* tailored to the interests of each individual reader. All of these technologies contribute to a media environment in which relatively specialized content is correlated with specific channels.

Channels Are Differentially Available

As the new media emerge, the assumption that mass media are universally available will become increasingly hollow. To be sure, owning a television set may continue to provide access to some common realm of programming, but that will constitute only a portion of what is consumed by the public. Much of what is consumed will be delivered through channels that are differentially available across the audience. The more choices available, the less likely it is that viewers will be exposed to the same selection of content.

This phenomenon of differential availability occurs as a result of technological, economic, and regulatory factors. Consider the case of cable television. The economics of cabling are such that it is unprofitable to wire areas that are sparsely populated. Even if the potential subscribers could pay the going rate for service, there are too few of them for cable companies to recover the costs of constructing the distribution system. Barring direct government subsidies, or a kind of utility regulation that allows cross-sub-sidization, people in these areas will have to resort to extraordinary means to gain access to the channels available to cable subscribers.

Even in areas that are cabled, the differential availability of channels is, at least in the short-term, a fact of life. Cable systems have varying channel capacities and may therefore be unable to carry all the cable networks that viewers desire. Systems with no practical limit in capacity often bundle channels into levels or *tiers* of service, making classes of channels available only for a premium (Wildman & Owen, 1985). Finally, of course, about 40% of the households that are passed by a cable may, for reasons of cost or preference, simply decline to subscribe.

Although alternative delivery systems such as *satellite reception dishes, multipoint distribution systems,* and VCRs do not exhibit the same limiting factors as cable, they carry their own technical limitations and impose their own sets of costs. It appears, then, that the net effect of the new technologies will be to make channels, and the kinds of content they carry, differentially available to the public.

Far from being the uniform and inescapable presence so often portrayed in media theory, the new media seem capable of recreating what we think of as "television" in a different form. It seems reasonable to expect that the medium will offer increasingly diverse programming, that this material will tend to be organized in channels specializing in relatively homogeneous forms of content, and that these channels will be available to some, but not all members of the public. Furthermore, it is worth noting that this evolution does not assume any changes in the motivation of either media owners or their audiences. Quite the contrary, change occurs because entrepreneurs continue to seek profits, and viewers continue to seek programming.

THE MASS AUDIENCE IN THE NEW MEDIA ENVIRONMENT

How these new media might alter the social impact of television or the need for various public policies will depend, in large measure, on how the audience responds to the changing environment. Will people sample widely from the diverse media materials laid before them? Will they continue to view only mass appeal programming, or will they consume relatively heavy doses of specialized content? To begin answering these questions, we turn our attention to two features of mass audience behavior that are especially sensitive to the changing character of mass media we have just described. The first, audience fragmentation, has to do with how the total audience is distributed across available channels. The second, audience polarization, addresses the intensity with which individuals or audience subsets use specific classes of media content.

Audience Fragmentation

The most widely anticipated and well-documented effect of new media on mass behavior is audience fragmentation. There has been a marked increase in the number of media-related choices confronting the audience, and these choices have divided the audience into smaller and smaller subsets. The fact that many of these channels are owned by a smaller number of parent corporations is of relatively little import for understanding mass behavior. Each service acts like a competitor, laying claim to some portion of the time people spend consuming media.

Table 7.1 provides a simple overview of how Americans allocate their time across a wide range of media. It shows estimates of the number of hours the average person spends consuming media in the course of a year. A few cautions about this table are in order. First, the data are collected from a number of research services. Although the column of hours is presented as additive, these activities may sometimes overlap. We know from research (Barwise & Ehrenberg, 1988; Bechtel, Achelpohl, & Akers, 1972), as well as our own experience, that television viewing is often low-involvement and accompanied by other forms of media use (e.g., reading). Second, these are broad national averages. There is undoubtedly great variation in how each individual allocates time across these categories. Finally, this is a snapshot of media use in the mid-1990s. Radio listening and newspaper reading have declined slightly over the years. Total television viewing has grown somewhat, as has the use of recorded music, home video games, and online computer services. All of these trends are expected to continue in the future. Overall media use is also expected to grow, but with the various categories already totaling more than 9 hours a day, we will surely encounter a ceiling effect before too long.

Bearing these caveats in mind, a couple of observations seem warranted. Television and radio totally dominate the time Americans spend with media. We suspect this is true wherever broadcast media are universally available to a mass audience. Whether these percentages offer a rough metric of the social impact of these media is harder to say. But it is certainly plausible, and if so, this would justify the disproportionate attention that television receives in media theory. Obviously, the lesser-used media include many newcomers. To the extent that Americans have already allocated about as many hours as possible to the media, audience attention to these newer media probably comes at the expense of older media. All this contributes to the general phenomenon of audience fragmentation.

TABLE 7.1
Hours Per Person Per Year Using Media

	Hours	Percent
Television	1,560	45.9%
Radio	1,102	32.4%
Recorded music	294	8.6%
Daily newspapers	169	5.0%
Consumer books	102	3.0%
Consumer magazines	84	2.5%
Home video	52	1.5%
Home video games	22	0.6%
Movies in theaters	12	0.4%
Online/Internet access	3	0.1%
Educational software	2	0.1%
TOTAL	3,402	100.0%

Source: Veronis, Suhler, and Associates, 1995.

What Table 7.1 does not reveal is how the dominant medium, television, has itself become internally fragmented. Indirect evidence of audience fragmentation has been apparent for some time through year-to-year comparisons of the combined audience share of the broadcast networks. In 1975, the three major U.S. networks commanded 90% of all the time the audience spent watching prime-time television. By 1994, that combined share had gradually dropped to 64% (Veronis, Suhler, & Associates, 1995). The missing 26% was presumably spread across independents, public stations, and cable services that had all grown in number and strength in the intervening years. At other times of the day, losses in audience share have been even more pronounced (Cabletelevision Advertising Bureau, 1995).

A clearer picture of audience fragmentation can be seen in a side-by-side comparison of noncable and cable households. Problems of self-selection aside, these modes of television reception embody many of the qualities of old and new media, respectively. Table 7.2 summarizes how the total national audience in each reception type distributed its weekly viewing in the 1993/1994 television season. As one would expect, noncable households allocated all their viewing to local, over-the-air, channels. Among cable households, the picture was different. More than 40% of all the time cable households spent watching television was devoted to cable channels of one sort or another.

What is not entirely clear from these data is whether the use of cable channels has reduced the amount of time viewers spend watching local stations or simply represents new viewing time added to the audience's daily diet of television. If broadcasters are, in effect, getting a smaller piece of a bigger pie, then some of their concern about audience erosion may be overblown (e.g., Park, 1979). Certainly, it is the case that cable and, especially, pay-cable homes watch more television than other households (Nielsen Media Research, 1993; Webster, 1983), but such data do not allow unambiguous causal inferences. We are more inclined to think that old media are simply getting a smaller piece of the same pie. As shown in chapter 2, a fairly substantial body of research and theory suggests that total television use is not determined by the combined drawing power of available content, but is fixed by exogenous factors (e.g., Barnett et al., 1991; Barwise, Ehrenberg, & Goodhardt, 1982; Webster & Wakshlag, 1983). This means that additional program options do not necessarily translate into more time spent viewing. Rather, they are more likely to prompt a reconfiguration of how audiences allocate their time. Under these circumstances, fragmentation would pose a greater threat to old media, although, as noted in chapter 3, the economic consequences of this erosion are far from obvious (e.g., Wirth & Bloch, 1985).

Generally speaking, the phenomenon of fragmentation is a function of the number and strength of channel options available to viewers. For example, pay-cable subscribers are known to distribute their viewing more widely than are basic-cable subscribers (Webster, 1983). Across the entire audience, then, as more people subscribe to new media systems, and as the systems to which people already subscribe expand their services, fragmentation is likely to increase. Furthermore, although good data are currently hard to come by, it seems probable that rapid growth in VCR-equipped households will facilitate the general trend toward fragmentation.

It is also clear, however, that not all channels contribute equally to the fragmentation of an audience. Introducing a third broadcast network signal into a market that previously had two will certainly have a more dramatic

TABLE 7.2
Audience Shares in Cable and Non-Cable Households

	Cable HH	Non-Cable HH
Total Broadcast	59	100
Network Affiliates	41	64
Independents	15	30
Public	3	6
Total Cable	41	
Basic	34	
Pay	7	
TOTAL TV	100%	100%

Source: Cabletelevision Advertising Bureau, 1995.

effect on how the local audience distributes its viewing, than adding a 35th new cable network to the local CATV system. Although this may be intuitively obvious, it is worth considering why it is so.

The broadcast network signal will, excepting vagaries in local geography, be accessible in virtually all homes. Under the circumstances just described, it would not be implausible for our hypothetical network to attract about a third of the available audience (e.g., perhaps 20% of all households might watch it during prime time). Conversely, the impact of a new cable network would be confined to those households that are in the cable system's franchise area and have subscribed to a bundle of services that include that network. If it has specialized programming, it may appeal to a small segment of the already reduced cable universe. In fact, even the most popular cable networks rarely have a prime time rating of more than 2 (i.e., on average 2% of cable households are watching). The differential availability of channels, therefore, circumscribes each one's potential for fragmenting the total audience. Because of these and other factors, any one cable network is unlikely to have a dramatic impact on total audience fragmentation. Nevertheless, the total audiences diverted from old media by cable, VCRs, and other new media may be substantial indeed.

Audience fragmentation, then, is a feature of aggregate audience behavior that occurs in response to the increased availability of channels. It has important implications for the viability of new media and the economic well-being of older media. To the degree that attendance to new media curtails the ability of the broadcast networks to command vast heterogeneous audiences at any point in time, fragmentation may also have larger social implications. Certainly the ability of television to provide society with some common ground, a core of shared experiences, has been an important aspect of the medium's presumed power (Gerbner & Gross, 1976; Hirsch, 1982).

But audience fragmentation, however pronounced, is only part of the picture. It is a gross measure of media use that reveals little about how intensively individual channels are used over time. For example, does an overall market share of 5 result from everyone spending about 5% of their time watching a channel, or does it result from some subset of the audience devoting larger portions of time to the channel? To more fully understand the impact of new media, we must consider a less-understood feature of mass behavior, audience polarization.

Audience Polarization

Audience polarization is the tendency of individuals to move to the extremes of either consuming or avoiding some class of media content. Such classes could include different genres of popular culture (e.g., recorded music, books, movies, etc.) They could be television programs defined by similarities in content, the channel on which they are telecast, or whatever dimensions are theoretically relevant. To the extent that one subset of the audience comes to use that class of content whereas others tend not to use it, the mass audience can be said to have polarized. The uniform, universally available quality of the old media has, for the most part, made audience polarization a moot point. The characteristics of new media, however, could produce significant levels of polarization. Broadly speaking, two factors are associated with the emergence of this phenomenon: content, and the structures through which content is delivered.

Theoretically, the availability of relatively diverse content will facilitate audience polarization. As we noted earlier, both uses and gratifications theories and economic models of program choice assume audience members have consistent preferences for content of a type. Similarly, most theories of selective exposure to communication predict that choice will be systematically related to content characteristics (e.g., Zillmann & Bryant, 1985). All other things being equal, as the media become more diversified, it should be easier for people to find content that more closely conforms to their preferences and avoid content that does not.

This seems to characterize a good deal of our media consumption already. It appears that people have powerful loyalties to some types of music and/or powerful aversions to others. It is easy to imagine people who read only certain types of books or magazines, attend only certain kinds of movies, and partake of rather specialized content from the Internet. All this bespeaks a considerable audience polarization. In the absence of countervailing forces, it could mean a growing tendency for people to consume media that portrays social reality in accordance with their own world views, a systematic avoidance of what they consider irrelevant or irreverent, and differential consumption of media with distinct ethnic appeals. Were it not for the mass medium of television providing a kind of ballast, modern society might founder. But television too is changing. As television critic Tom Shales noted at the beginning of the decade:

> Everything is ending. Nothing is beginning. Television as we have known it is unraveling, and when the strands and threads are put back together, it may be all but unrecognizable. . . . For forty years we were one nation indivisible, under television. That's ending. Television is turning into something else, and so are we. We're different. We're splintered. We're not as much "we" as the "we" we were. We're divisible. (cited in Dizard, 1994, p. 102)

A critical question, then, is how much audience polarization will occur in the medium of television. It should be noted at this point that, theoretical expectations aside, the actual tendency of television audiences to systematically watch or not watch content of a type is far from overwhelming. In fact, Goodhardt et al. (1987) reported that there is no special tendency for people who watch one program to seek out other programs of the same genre. It may be that the low-involvement nature of television viewing (Barwise & Ehrenberg, 1988), as well as deeply ingrained habits of media use (Neuman, 1991) predisposes the audience to consume a fairly broad range of mass appeal programs. However, it may also be that the apparent lack of program-type loyalties in television viewing are predetermined by the structure of the old media environment. Certainly we have seen that program-type effects are limited by a number of factors, including the scheduling characteristics of conventional broadcast television. As the structure of the media environment changes, it may promote rather than confound program-type effects, leading to more pronounced levels of audience polarization.

This leads us to the second factor that has been associated with audience polarization—the structure through which program content is delivered. Channel loyalty, sometimes called a network effect, is a longstanding and commonly observed feature of television audience behavior (Bruno, 1973; Goodhardt et al., 1987). As we noted elsewhere, it is the tendency of programs on the same channel to have a disproportionately large dupli-cated audience. In other words, audiences are known to polarize around programs defined by the channel on which they are telecast. Why this happens is not entirely clear. During a single viewing session, it may result from several factors including a kind of "attention inertia" (Anderson & Lorch, 1983; Webster, 1985). On a day-to-day basis, Darmon (1976) specu-lated that such loyalty may, in fact, be a function of program content, although others (e.g., Goodhardt et al., 1987) discount that explanation.

In any event, the very label of channel loyalty implies that a segment of the audience affirmatively seeks out a channel. In fact, a similar result would occur if some subset of the audience systematically avoided a channel. To the extent that new media channels are differentially available to substantial segments of the audience, the potential for a kind of de facto polarization is considerable. That is, audiences would move to the extremes of channel use and nonuse, not for reasons of preference, but because they are physically precluded from membership in the channel's audience. Such a potentially powerful determinant of polarization has not been contem-plated by most audience analysts because television channels have been so easily conceptualized as universally available.

Although either factor alone (e.g., content or structure) could produce audience polarization, in new media environments, content and channels tend to be correlated. This is a situation ripe with possibilities for moving channel audiences to the extremes of use and nonuse. It also raises interest-ing questions about the patterns of audience behavior that may underlie the audience fragmentation described in the previous section. For example, do such overall patterns imply that each individual's viewing time is similarly distributed, or do they mask considerable variation from person to person?

Webster (1989) explored this question by analyzing television diary data collected in a large city in the southwestern United States. The market had a typical complement of five broadcast stations, including an independent that offered Spanish-language programming. Each of the local affiliates was watched at some point in the week by the overwhelming majority of the market population. The ABC station, for example, was seen by 85% of the sample and, across the entire market, commanded a 27% share of audience. Furthermore, among those who watched the station at all, it occupied 30% of their viewing time. The other affiliates exhibited the same general pattern of audience shares. Beyond these traditional purveyors of mass appeal programming, however, the patterns of audience behavior changed.

The Spanish independent station had, overall, a 6% share of the audience. In this case, however, only 16% of the population tuned into the station in the course of a week. But among the people who did tune in, they spent almost 40% of their time with the station. For this subset of the audience, then, the Spanish station was a more substantial presence than any one of the network affiliates. Such intensity of use is not apparent in conventional market shares. It is also contrary to the double jeopardy phenomenon we reviewed in chapter 5. In this case, polarization appears to have been a function of preference for content because, as a broadcast signal, structural barriers to station use were minimal.

The audience for cable channels also shows signs of polarization, although here structural considerations make the causes more difficult to identify. Certainly, overall shares and circulation are limited by subscription to cable. Nevertheless, the differential availability of channels cannot completely explain their audience shares. In the case of more specialized services, it appears that some special appetite for content also drives polarization (Barnes, 1990). Among the audience subsets who do use specialized channels, it is a relatively substantial item in their diet of television programming. For example, research on music videos indicates very intense use of such services among otherwise limited audiences (Sun & Lull, 1986). The determination of underlying causes for audience polarization, then, is a more complicated calculus when structural factors are taken into account.

Underlying the broad patterns of audience fragmentation described in the preceding section are various subpatterns of audience polarization. Although the total audience is more widely distributed than ever before, that does not necessarily mean that individuals spread their viewing across an equally wide range of sources. Indeed, Heeter and Greenberg (1985) argued that even cable subscribers limit their viewing to a relative handful, or repertoire, of preferred channels. It seems likely that VCRs will only increase the tendency to watch or avoid classes of programs (Dobrow, 1990; Levy, 1989). As television becomes more diverse and structurally complex, people will have created, sometimes by default, media environments that can be quite different from those of their neighbors. In the aggregate, this manifests itself as both audience fragmentation and polarization.

Just how far these emerging features of audience behavior will go remains to be seen. Although this chapter has cast audience behavior as a response to changes in the media environment, we do not mean to endorse a simple kind of "technological determinism." In reality, the structure of the media is both cause and effect. If individuals demonstrate an appetite for continuous doses of relatively specialized kinds of content, particularly if they are willing to pay a premium for such material, then the industry will surely oblige them and increased levels of polarization will result. If, as Ehrenberg (1986) argued, viewers have a demand for range in programming, then more modest levels of polarization, probably attributable to structural factors, will occur.

Although we expect that the new media environment will allow for increased levels of both audience fragmentation and polarization, when it comes to television, we are inclined to ally ourselves with more conservative forecasters (e.g., Barwise & Ehrenberg, 1988; Eastman & Newton, 1995; Neuman, 1991). It is apparent from currently available data that traditional, mass appeal network television still dominates media consumption in the United States. That is not likely to change anytime soon. Of course, changes in patterns of exposure to the media need not be dramatic to be of real significance. As Gerbner et al. (1986) pointed out, a "slight but pervasive shift" in the audience's experience with a mass medium may have far-reaching cultural implications (p. 21). We consider some of those implications in chapter 8.

Furthermore, even if new media succeed in fragmenting the audience into countless, tiny, internally homogeneous subsets, it would not necessarily spell the demise of the mass audience. In the old media environment, we came to associate audiences with specific items of content consumed at specific points in time. In fact, *simultaneous delivery* has long been part of the textbook definition of mass communications. But there is nothing inherent in the mass audience concept that requires this temporal restriction. As we indicated in chapter 3, advertisers and some program syndicators can claim to reach a mass audience by adding together viewership over several runs of a program. In effect, they reconstitute a mass audience by aggregating it across time. This suggests that when the assumption of simultaneous viewing is eliminated, even fairly esoteric media content might accumulate a large audience. At the very least, we can expect mass merchandisers will continue constructing mass audiences for their commercial messages.

Chapter 8

The Mass Audience
in Media Theory

Conceiving of the audience as a mass is common practice for media industries and most other social institutions. Since the earliest days of advertiser support, this model has been indispensable for turning the audience into a salable commodity. The pursuit of a mass audience has, in turn, guided the actions of publishers and programmers. Simple measures of audience size and composition have also been central in orchestrating all manner of media campaigns, whether the purpose is to sell soap or political candidates. Even the new media environment, which may change our vocabulary from "mass to market" (McQuail, 1994), hardly alters the fundamentals of mass audience thinking. Despite the ebb and flow of theoretical fashions in the academy, in practice, the idea of a mass audience has dominated how we think of audiences and will probably do so in the years to come.

Considering this dominant position, there is a surprisingly limited scholarly literature on the mass audience. There is, as we have seen, a good deal of applied work on mass audience behavior in marketing research. This tends to be quite technical and rarely engages larger social or cultural issues. There are also a number of ad hoc studies of the audience dating back to the early work of Paul Lazarsfeld (Webster, in press). Because the mass audience is so essential to understanding the operation of media industries, the construct receives a good deal of attention in both critical and traditional studies of media economics. But for the most part, this concept, which is so central to industry practice, is often marginalized or simply ignored in contemporary media theory. Consider, for example, a wide-ranging review of audience studies by Jensen and Rosengren (1990). The authors claim to identify and compare the "main research traditions examining the nexus between media and audiences" (p. 207). These traditions include everything from effects research to literary criticism. Curiously, there is nothing but the most fleeting reference to mainstream audience research and the tradition of aggregating behavior to determine how real audiences come into contact with real media systems. Our purpose in this chapter is to explore how the concept of a mass audience is, or could be, applied in media theory. We consider three broad areas of scholarly work: effects research, cultural studies, and media policy.

MEDIA EFFECTS

Determining how mass media influence society has been a recurring concern of the communications discipline from its inception (Lowery & De-Fleur, 1987). Katz and Lazarsfeld (1955) argued that the study of media effects, broadly defined, was the "over-riding interest of mass media research" (pp. 18–19). Even among those who would have the discipline turn to other areas, there is a general recognition that the study of media effects is largely responsible for the existence of communications as an academic enterprise (Jensen & Rosengren, 1990; Rogers, 1994). Determining what media do to people has been, and will continue to be a central concern of media theory (Bryant & Zillmann, 1994; Wartella, in press).

The advertising industry, of course, has been in the business of managing media effects and shaping public opinion for some time. Given the pivotal role that data on the mass audience play in directing media campaigns, one might imagine that the concept of a mass audience was an essential feature of academic theory on media effects. That is not the case. We suspect this is because many theorists wrongly equate a mass audience with a passive audience.

Down With the Passive Mass

The academic study of media effects is sufficiently long and central to the discipline that it has developed a kind of official history (Pietila, 1994). It is a story told time and again in countless books and articles. In essence, it stipulates that the first theorists to consider the effects of mass communication viewed the audience as an isolated mass of individuals easily manipulated by the media. This is a concept of mass society that is often attributed to the Frankfurt School (Beniger, 1987). Even today, one can scarcely read the term mass audience in the academic literature without finding the word passive appearing nearby, or somehow implied by the text. As the story goes, by the 1950s, wiser heads had determined that audience members were much more resistant to change than mass society theory suggested. The audience selectively perceived media messages and were held in place by a network of social relations. This model of the audience, sometimes called the *limited effects* perspective, became the dominant paradigm of the field (Gitlin, 1978).

The problem with this history is that it perpetuates a false equivalence between a mass audience and a passive, nonselective audience. At best, the mass audience is a necessary—but insufficient—condition for mass society to emerge. As noted in chapter 1, there is nothing in the concept of the mass, as it was first articulated by Blumer (1946), or in contemporary advertising practice that requires us to position the audience as a bunch of passive dolts. In fact, this construction of the mass audience is so implausible that several historians of the discipline have concluded it was nothing more than a straw man used to cast the limited effects model in sharper relief (Chaffee & Hochheimer, 1985; Czitrom, 1982; Pietila, 1994). At any rate, the damage was done. For many academics, the mass audience was forever associated with discredited notions of mass society. As Beniger (1987) observed, "by 1962, arguments centered on mass society seemed to reach exhaustion—it is difficult to find the term indexed in an American book after that year" (p. S51). Much of the discipline effectively threw out the baby with the bath water.

In our view, the mass audience concept is agnostic with regard to questions of audience passivity. It is simply a way to gauge who in the audience has come into contact with the media, thereby establishing certain parameters within which media effects may or may not emerge. As such, it could be applied with equal relevance to critical studies of media power or research that invests the audience with great powers of resistance and rationality. That has certainly been the case in discussions of media policy, a topic we address in a later section.

More recent scholarship has taken the limited effects model of the audience to task, suggesting that it overstates the power and autonomy of the audience. British cultural studies have criticized the dominant paradigm for being overly mechanical and insensitive to how people decode and use the media they encounter. There has also been a reemergence of critical theory that harkens back to the mass society model. As Katz (1987) noted:

> The boom in studies of audience decodings has almost overshadowed two pioneering empirical studies which operationalize a more classic critical stance, those of Gerbner and Gross (1976) and Noelle-Neumann (1973). These come, respectively from the Left and Right of the political spectrum (which means that a case can be made that the Right can also have a critical theory). Both studies assume a classical mass society in which the individual is atomized, locked into his home for fear of going out (Gerbner), or locked into silence for fear of being ostracized (Noelle-Neumann). (p. S32)

Many Out of One

Such popular theories offer an appropriate forum for a reconsideration of the mass audience and its applicability to media effects. A central tenet of these theories, and much contemporary research on the effects of television, is that the media are a pervasive and uniform presence in the lives of all members of society. Represented as such a monolithic entity, television has been readily conceptualized as the source of many significant social effects. Among these are the medium's ability to promote social integration and cultural uniformity (Neuman, 1982), cultivate political moderation (Gerbner, Gross, Morgan, & Signorielli, 1984) and distorted perceptions of social reality (Gerbner et al., 1986), facilitate a *spiral of silence* in the formation of public opinion (Noelle-Neumann, 1973), set broad societal agendas (McCombs & Shaw, 1972), and, more generally, to maintain a scheme of class stratification (Murdock & Golding, 1977).

The audience's response to the new media environment, however, raises questions about theories that continue to assume mass media are a uniform presence in the lives of all people. Not only are the new media themselves more diverse, but individual audience members seem to exploit that diversity to create increasingly unique media environments for themselves. Out of one mass, the media may produce or sustain many *publics*. This implies certain changes in how social effects will transpire.

Audience fragmentation suggests that there is a decreasing probability that any two people will have read the same magazine article or even seen the same program on television on a given evening. This might, in some way, alter the social utility of media content as a common "coin of exchange." Conversely, this same phenomenon raises the possibility that advertising messages, which span the entire medium, could take on added salience as topics of conversation and definers of popular culture.

More importantly, the trend toward audience polarization suggests that there may be long-term, systematic differences in the kinds of content to which different segments of the population are exposed. Traditional forms of television enforced a certain breadth of exposure on viewers. Ironically, it is only in more diverse media environments that individuals can consume relatively narrow regimens of content. Might such polarization in the consumption of media content ultimately produce analogous kinds of *social polarization*?

Even if the use of specialized channels or program content does not dominate an individual's viewing time, it is conceivable that it may wield a disproportionate influence on the viewer. Minority language programming, for example, may be especially effective in forming perceptions of social reality, setting agendas, or maintaining the cultural identity of those who watch it (Dobrow, 1989; Rodriguez, 1996). All these possibilities warrant further investigation by effects researchers.

The Presumed Audience

The traditional form of the effects question asks, what do media do to people? But that is not the only way media effects can be conceived. In chapter 1, we suggested that the mass audience was invested with certain powers that could affect institutional conduct. We might, therefore, ask, what does the mass audience do to institutions? With the exception of work that conceives of mass audience behavior as a feedback mechanism to industry (e.g., McDonald & Schechter, 1988; Owen & Wildman, 1992), this is an area that is very much undertheorized. We offer here some speculations on what we call the effects of a *presumed audience*.

In chapter 1, we noted that the Panopticon had become a popular metaphor for describing institutional control over the audience (Ang, 1991; Gandy, 1993; Herbst, 1993). The central authority looks out on the masses. Because people are never quite certain if their actions are being watched, they come to internalize acceptable standards of conduct. But imagine that the sight lines of the Panopticon are reversed. The guard in the central tower is observed by a thousand eyes that encircle him. He knows they are there, but he cannot see them. To us, this seems the more apt model of the mass audience. Public figures and institutions take center stage. They believe they are being watched, although they are never quite sure by whom. The presumed audience, envisioned as an unseen mass, exerts a coercive force on those being observed.

There is a good deal of anecdotal evidence that attests to the power of a presumed audience. In 1968, as America's involvement in Vietnam grew, the Democratic Party met in Chicago to nominate a Presidential candidate. Antiwar activists by the thousands flooded the city, mounting one protest after another. In what was later described as a police riot, demonstrators were clubbed and dragged off to jail. Network cameras, looking down on the mayhem in the streets, broadcast the event. The demonstrators, cognizant of the cameras, began to chant "the whole world is watching,"—invoking the power of the mass audience as a defense against institutions run amuck.

It seems clear to us that such presumed audiences exert real pressure on public forums and figures. But the idea of this audience is usually buried in more complex notions about the power of the press. Consider, for example, one of the seminal works on media influence. Lazarsfeld and Merton (1948) identified several social functions of the mass media. Among these were *status conferral* and the enforcement of *social norms*. In the former, the media are thought to legitimize or elevate the status of people or institutions by selecting them as the object of their attention. In the latter, the media are believed to promote conformism by publicizing conditions at variance with social norms. Lazarsfeld and Merton attributed much of the power of the media to confer status or enforce norms to the layman's respect for the editorial judgment of experts (e.g., "If *The New York Times* thinks this is important, it must be"). We are inclined to believe, however, that the presumption that a mass audience is in attendance is the more potent determinant of these social effects. Editors may direct the spotlight that brings things to public attention, but the mass of the audience determines the brightness of the light.

The notion of a presumed audience raises many questions. Who makes these presumptions? On what basis? How do they influence the actions that follow? Certainly, institutions in the public spotlight are aware of media audiences. They are also in a position to quantify these audiences, although it is less clear that empiricism always informs the actions of the organization. The case of the individual viewer is harder yet to unravel. It is likely that people watching a media event know that a vast audience is in attendance. Such awareness is part of the event's appeal, and the media are generally eager to report the estimated worldwide audience. That knowledge undoubtedly enhances the event's utility as a common cultural referent. Like the weather, it becomes something we can all talk about.

What individuals presume about the audience for more ordinary fare is an open question. Some social theories imply that people are cognizant of the audience for a message. *Third person effects* are a case in point. According to Davison (1983), the recipient of a message generally believes him or herself to be immune from its effect. However, people readily assume that other "third persons" exposed to the message are affected. The belief that others are affected, in turn, shapes the behavior of those who think themselves immune. Obviously, the theory of third person effects requires a presumption of audience among individuals. If we believe that each person is oblivious to the possible audience for a message, there would be no reason for third person effects to materialize. Conversely, it is plausible that if people ascribe a large audience to the message, third person effects will grow accordingly. Other social theories, like the spiral of silence (Noelle-Neumann, 1984), imply that individuals have some innate quasi-statistical sensibility.

Until quite recently, it was probably reasonable for institutions and individuals, as well as social theorists, to assume that all media had mass audiences. This simplifying assumption dropped the notion of a presumed audience from the equation by making it a kind of theoretical constant. So, for instance, if something was on television, it went without saying that it had a large, heterogeneous audience. As the mass audience becomes increasingly fragmented, we may need to be more explicit about the place of audience, presumed or otherwise, in the social functions of media.

CULTURAL STUDIES

One of the things that attracted us to a book about the mass audience was a growing interest in audience theory among students of cultural studies. We would be remiss if we did not consider how mass audience thinking might engage critical scholarship. Frankly, we do so with some hesitation.

Proponents of a critical perspective are often unsympathetic to mainstream audience research. Consider, for example, Ang's (1991) critique of Good-hardt et al. (1975):

> Applying advanced statistical techniques, the authors have managed to construct a dazzling range of curious forms of aggregated audience behavior, such as 'audience flow,' 'repeat-viewing,' and 'channel loyalty.' Their mathematical *tour de force* leads the authors to conclude that 'instead of being complex . . . viewing behavior and audience appreciation appear to follow a few general and simple patterns operating right across the board.' As a result, Goodhardt, et al. claim to be capable of mapping audience behaviour with all but law-like precision. . . . In this instance the streamlining process has become all but complete: 'television audience' is reduced almost entirely to a set of objective regularities, and seems to be more or less completely purged from any subjective peculiarities in people's engagements with television. (p. 156)

If our only purpose in studying the audience is to ferret out the "subjective peculiarities" of people's media use, if we have no interest in the generalizability of our findings, then perhaps it is wrong-headed to consider any linkage between cultural studies and the mass audience concept. We noted elsewhere that mass audience thinking focuses heavily on exposure to media while offering few, if any, insights into the meaning of media use. Perhaps that limitation alone should preempt further discussion. After all, Hall (1980) argued that "if no 'meaning' is taken, there can be no 'consumption'" (p. 128). We believe, however, that patterns of exposure to media ought to interest critical scholars, and we offer as a counterpoint to Hall's observation that if no consumption occurs, there is nothing to take meaning from. At any rate, we suggest, for the reader's consideration, the following points of contact between the mass audience perspective and cultural studies.

Audience Differentiation

Increasingly, cultural studies makes reference to different human collectivities. These are variously referred to as *subcultures, interpretive communities,* taste publics, and so forth. Oftentimes, the research that discovers these groups is cast in opposition to mainstream audience research:

> Reception and ethnographic research have demonstrated that the mass audience is significantly heterogeneous, not only in relation to gender, class, culture, and age, but also in relation to cognitions, involvement, and styles of viewing. In short, the "mass" of mass communications has been challenged, and theories and methods must adapt. (Livingstone, 1993, p. 9)

This kind of posturing perpetuates a falsehood about the mass audience. As noted in chapter 1, there is nothing in the theory or practice of mass audience thinking that discourages *audience differentiation*. In fact, it has been a mainstay of this type of research. Although the vocabulary used for describing the audience may vary by discipline, the notions of taste public and market segment have much in common. Each identifies some subset of the mass, often on the basis of their social standing or the media they consume. Each is an aggregation of individuals, frequently unknown to one another, who are identified by the researcher for his or her own purposes. In fact, Moores (1993) noted that Bourdieu's method for investigating the sociology of taste "resembles one which is used nowadays by commercial market researchers in 'psychographic' consumer surveys" (p. 119). With the growth of new media, offering specialized content to narrowly targeted populations, interest in disaggregating the mass is likely to grow. To us, this raises the possibility of overlapping interests for which data on the mass audience might be of some value to students of popular culture.

Of course, we should not expect a complete convergence of interests. Turow (1984) noted that ratings companies measure audience categories that "directly reflect the specific marketing concerns of sponsors" (p. 147), and that these may fail to represent relevant publics. In a similar vein, Peterson (1994) observed that media industries sometimes concoct market categories that do not conform to the real desires and interests of the audience. Nonetheless, it would be quite odd if the categories that interest mass merchandisers bore no relationship to the tastes and interpretive capabilities of the audience.

Demographic factors, such as age, gender, income, and race, are staples of market segmentation in mass audience research. Although such individual traits should not be thought of as simple causes of cultural competence, they can still reveal something about a person's place in the social structure, and so bear on their reading of the media. As Morely (1985) argued, "individuals in different positions in the social formation defined according to structures of class, race, or sex, for example, will tend to inhabit or have at their disposal different codes and subcultures. This social position sets parameters to potential readings by structuring access to different codes" (pp. 239–240). Gans (1974) and Bourdieu (1984) also noted strong relationships among demographic factors and taste cultures.

Demographics, however, offer only one way of differentiating the mass audience. A number of other approaches may offer equally useful insights. The high visibility of network ratings sometimes obscures the existence of local audience measurement. During a nationwide ratings "sweep," a ratings company will collect over 100,000 diaries (Webster & Wakshlag, 1985). Such vast samples permit reliable geographic comparisons among regions of the country and, sometimes, relatively fine comparisons in cities.

In fact, it is increasingly common to analyze differences in media consumption by postal zip codes. By melding demographic and geographic variables, marketing research companies have created tightly drawn market segments with such provocative labels as "Furs & Station Wagons" or "Shotguns & Pickups" (Larson, 1992). If one believes that these map onto interpretive communities, they may provide another window on the workings of popular culture. Moores (1993) suggested just such a possibility.

Jensen (1987) argued that among the critical elements in the reception process are "situational factors," and that to understand the "lived reality behind the ratings," we need to study the context of media usage (p. 25). It is rarely considered, but unprocessed ratings data contain a good deal of information about that context. Diaries and certain meter data, for instance, track what configuration of family members and visitors view household televisions. Although these data do not offer the rich insights of ethnographic work, they can help us understand, in a general way, where and with whom particular media materials are consumed.

In administering the *coup de grace* of her critique of Goodhardt et al. (1975), Ang chastised the authors for imputing preferences, or a lack thereof, from accounts of viewing behavior. Rather, Ang (1991) pointed to the mediating influence of family members as the factor that accounts for this phenomenon and subverts "the decontextualized, one-dimensional definition of 'television watching'" (p. 157). She cited Morely (1986) as the principal authority for this finding. Ironically, Morely himself cited a secondary analysis of commercially collected television viewing diaries (Webster & Wakshlag, 1982) as the source of his insights on the impact of group viewing. These are exactly the same kind of data used by Goodhardt et al. to document patterns of viewing. Obviously, for anyone willing to look, the data are capable of offering a range of insights.

Perhaps the most effective and relevant way to differentiate the mass audience is by the media materials they actually consume. Gans (1974) noted that, ultimately, membership in a taste public is expressed in one's choice of the available cultural offerings. Similarly, Radway (1985) referred to reading a specific category of books as being suggestive of a person's place in an interpretive community. With their focus on how and when people come into contact with media, data on the mass audience can tell us a good deal about the nexus between popular culture and the audience. In their simplest form they can document what cultural products are, in fact, popular—and with whom. Shepard (1986), for example, produced a map describing the consumption of music among young Canadians. In their more complex applications, audience data allow us to learn something about a person's diet of mass media over time. A case in point is audience flow. In the section that follows, we specifically consider how studies of audience duplication can illuminate the construction of media texts.

Flow Texts

Raymond Williams (1974) was among the first to argue that individual television programs do not exist as discrete entities in the minds of viewers. Rather, a kind of flow across texts is the "central experience" of the medium (p. 95)—a fact that accounts for much of television's critical significance. This flow occurs both in a day's viewing, and across the episodes of a series. Noting this, Newcombe and Hirsch (1984) argued that our notions of the television text need redefinition. Rather than analyze individual programs, *viewing strips* or *flow texts* ought to be studied, as these more nearly reflect the experience of viewing.

Yet, how are the appropriate flow texts to be identified? Certainly some scheduling configurations make one sequencing of texts more likely than another. But it is the audience member who ultimately determines the ordering of texts. How do audiences actually move across the programming at their disposal? The patterns of audience duplication we reported in earlier chapters offer one, empirically grounded, way to address these questions.

Repeat viewing, the reader will recall, is the extent to which people return to watch succeeding episodes in a series of programs. It is widely believed that a person who becomes a fan of a particular program will watch it with great regularity. In fact, levels of repeat viewing are quite low. Even among the soap opera audience—described in popular lore as the most loyal of viewers—a good 45% of those who see one episode do not see the next. Over the long haul, this means that many of a program's viewers see less than half of its episodes. For example, 60% of London's adult population saw the critically acclaimed program *Brideshead Revisited*. Of these viewers, less than a third saw a majority of the eleven episodes. An equal number saw just one episode, and a scant 3% saw them all (Goodhardt et al., 1987, p. 62). Textual analyses that assume a regular acquaintance with plot lines or characters and their development, may seriously overstate the facts of viewer experience.

Inheritance effects are another pattern of audience duplication that bears on the formation of flow texts. We know that there is a tendency for the audience of one program to be overrepresented in the audience of the program that follows. This feature of audience flow is common knowledge among programmers and media analysts. However, the popular notion that an audience can be captured for an entire evening is overblown. During prime time, for example, about half of a program's audience will stay tuned for the following program. Beyond adjacent programs, inheritance effects dissipate rapidly. Organizing a flow text that assumes most viewers stick with a channel through an entire evening is similarly at odds with viewer experience.

Of course, changes in the media environment may make channels a more salient organizing principle of audience behavior. As we have seen, a growing correlation of content and channel, as well as the differential availability of those channels, promotes a degree of audience polarization. Ethnic channels, in particular, appear to have small but unusually loyal audiences. Viewers of music video, sports, and religious channels exhibit similar, if less pronounced, loyalties. All this suggests that simplistic notions of mass audiences consuming mass quantities of undifferentiated mass produced programming are inadequate. Students of popular culture might actually find audience data a useful guide to increasingly varied and idiosyncratic patterns of media consumption.

Unfortunately, some proponents of cultural studies view the mass audience concept and the data it produces as having only limited and predetermined institutional applications. They would have us believe there is just one way to read the mass audience. This is an odd position for scholars who have done so much to demonstrate that media texts are subject to multiple readings. Audience information is polysemic as well. When confronting ratings data, a programmer may see something quite different than a media buyer or a government policymaker. So too might a student of popular culture. Far from being an impoverished text with a preordained meaning, we believe that mass audience data are rich in interpretive possibilities.

MEDIA POLICY

Perhaps the most fascinating applications of mass audience thinking are in the general area of media policy. It is here that many of the themes we developed in this book resonate and coalesce. It seems appropriate, therefore, to end with a discussion of the mass audience in media policy.

Since the earliest days of broadcasting, the official goal of American policy has been to ensure service in the *public interest* (Federal Radio Commission, 1928). More often than not, the public is conceived of as a large collection of citizens, unknown to each other and unseen by government—except, perhaps, as poll data. This concept of the public bears obvious similarities to the mass audience. In fact, Herbst and Beniger (1994), argued that contemporary notions of the public have become largely interchangeable with the idea of audience.

In the case of media policy, however, the mass audience is imbued with a range of traits that are not always seen in other applications of the construct. Based on a review of several decades of court cases and federal regulations, Webster and Phalen (1994) identified three variations of the dominant model commonly used by policymakers. Table 8.1 summarizes the distinguishing characteristics of each submodel. All three are manifestations of mass audience thinking, yet each one portrays the audience in a

TABLE 8.1
Models of Audience in Communications Policy*

	Commodity Model "Audience as Value"	Effects Model "Audience as Victim"	Marketplace Model "Audience as Consumer"
Assumptions			
The Audience	The audience has an economic value that is expressed in measurements of its size and composition	Audience members are easily exposed to programming that may or may not be in their own best interest	Audience members are rational, well-informed individuals who will act in their own self-interest
Relationship Between Media and the Audience	Commercial media must be allowed to create and sell audiences if the media are to exist	Media can cultivate an appetite for vulgar, hateful, or trivial programming	Audience members come to the media with well-formed program preferences that cause them to choose specific content
The Public Interest	The public interest is served by preserving the system of advertiser supported media	The public interest is served by a media system that limits exposure to undesirable programming and promotes exposure to meritorious content	The public interest is served by a media system that is responsive to audience preferences as revealed in their viewing choices
Manifestations			
Focus of Regulation	Government concern for the economic well-being of established media	Content and ownership regulation	Deregulation
Examples in Law and Regulation**	Economic injury Syndicated exclusivity Compulsory copyright Must-carry	Radio format controversy Indecency Fairness Doctrine Ownership regulations	"Free Speech" Privatization Radio formats revisited
Rhetoric	Rhetoric of media "ownership" of audiences	Rhetoric of responsibility— moral, political	Rhetoric of marketplace—demand and supply

*Adapted from Webster & Phalen (1994). **Although each of these examples may be appropriately placed within a primary model, arguments often overlap.

very different light. We use this framework to structure the discussion that follows.

We believe that these are distinct, internally consistent models of the mass audience. We should be quick to point out, however, that this does not mean policymakers who invoke a particular model acknowledge it as such, or espouse it consistently over time. These are not clearly articulated audience paradigms, whose attributes are well-understood and recognized by all who use them. More often than not, ideas about the audience lurk just below the surface. They can exist as benign assumptions or as strategically crafted images intended to affect policy outcomes. Quite often, participants in the policy-making process will adopt whatever model allows them to advance their own interests while still paying homage to the public interest. This is especially true of the media themselves, who may characterize the audience as rational decision makers one moment and prospective victims the next. Such contradictory lines of argument are surprisingly difficult to detect. As we noted elsewhere "the fact that the same people use different models at different times has probably obscured the role of audience models in policy debates" (Webster & Phalen, 1994, p. 33). Whether they are easily discernible, we believe they are persistent and powerful determinants of media policy. Our purpose here is to draw them out so we can more fully consider their implications.

The Commodity Model

The idea that the audience is a commodity is already familiar to us. We have seen, especially in chapter 3, that audiences have considerable value to media industries. Each year, tens of billions of dollars are spent in hopes of capturing a piece of the mass audience. This fact of life has not eluded American policymakers. It is not unusual, therefore, to see laws and regulations that explicitly recognize the audience as a commodity.

One of the ways in which this model shows itself is in the government's long-standing concern over the economic well-being of established media. Although American broadcasters are private businesses, they are also obligated to serve the public interest. In order to do so, they must have sufficient resources. This role as public trustee has opened the door for a consideration of station revenues in policy debates. Although it may be unspoken, the mass audience is often at the heart of these discussions:

> To license two stations where there is revenue only for one may result in no good service at all. So economic injury to an existing station, while not in and of itself a matter of moment, becomes important when on the facts it spells the diminution or destruction of service. At that point the element of injury

ceases to be a matter of purely private concern. (*Carrol Broadcasting Company v. FCC*, 1958, p. 443)

This kind of reasoning has rationalized much government action. In the late 1960s and early 1970s, the Federal Communications Commission (FCC) set in place a number of policies that sharply limited the growth of cable television (LeDuc, 1987). The principle justification for these policies was that cable would divert audiences that were needed to sustain licensees (Park, 1979). Similarly, the government has enacted measures to protect the audience for syndicated programs sold to broadcasters. In announcing its policy on *syndicated exclusivity* the FCC reasoned, "the ability to limit diversion means broadcasters will be able to attract larger audiences, making them more attractive to advertisers, thereby enabling them to obtain more and better programming for their viewers" (The Why's and Wherefores of Syndex II, 1988, pp. 58–59).

In all of these applications, the government has shown few inhibitions about recognizing the commodity value of the audience. It may strike some as odd that civil servants would countenance the buying and selling of the public in the name of the public interest. Yet, that is effectively what happens. Moreover, public policies frequently assign the value of the audience to specific players in the process. It sometimes seems that broadcast licensees or copyright holders have been awarded a kind of property right in their audience.

The Effects Model

Quite apart from any consideration of economic value, it is common for policymakers to characterize the audience as the potential victim of the media. This concept of the audience is consistent with many long-standing traditions in effects research. It is probably also fair to say that this view of the audience conforms with what the "man in the street" believes about the power of the media. The effects model, then, draws both on academic theory and common sense, making it a potent tool for policymakers.

In essence, this model positions the audience as a passive lot, easily affected by the media. Although it is possible for the media to do good things for people, the concern of those who adopt this model more often centers on the bad things media are likely to do. In that regard, it comports rather well with mass society theory and its more contemporary manifestations (e.g., cultivation analysis, etc.). The general thrust of policy under this model is to limit exposure to undesirable programming and promote exposure to meritorious content.

In practice, this model works in a variety of ways. Its most obvious application is in regulations designed to protect the public from harmful content. Indecency, for example, has been forbidden from broadcasting in the belief that it has undesirable effects, especially on children. The problem is that any blanket prohibition runs afoul of the American commitment to freedom of speech and reduces the adult audience to hearing "only what is fit for children" (*Butler v. Michigan*, 1957, p. 383).

To strike a balance between these competing interests, the government has sought to confine indecency to *safe harbor* hours when children are not in the audience. In fact, the FCC has used ratings data to identify times when the child audience is at its lowest ebb (Webster, 1990). Unfortunately for policymakers, some number of children are always in the audience, making ironclad protections unattainable. But, given the impossibility of the task, channeling content away from the largest number of people at risk seems a reasonable way to minimize the adverse impact of harmful content.

A less obvious, although no less important, application of the effects model addresses victimization that results from the absence of good content. As we see in the audience model that follows, media policy in America has placed heavy reliance on a competitive marketplace to deliver the appropriate mix of programming to the public. Some policymakers have argued that this system fails to produce enough worthwhile content, thereby harming the public interest.

Nowhere is there a stronger statement of this position than in Newton Minow's *Vast Wasteland* speech of 1961—perhaps the most influential public statement ever made by a member of the FCC. He took for granted the "overwhelming impact" of broadcasting on the American people (Minow, 1978, p. 284). While acknowledging that there were a few good programs on television, Minow criticized commercial broadcasters for their pursuit of ever higher audience ratings and concluded that "if parents, teachers, and ministers conducted their responsibilities by following the ratings, children would have a steady diet of ice cream, school holidays, and no Sunday School" (Minow, 1978, p. 286). Throughout the course of his address, Minow made it clear that responding only to the demands of the mass audience is misguided—"some say that the public interest is merely what interests the public. I disagree" (p. 283).

This vision of the audience is not unique to the United States. It is similar to what one finds in government-owned media around the world. Ang (1991) labeled this the *audience-as-public* construct and described it in the following way:

> The audience-as-public consists not of consumers, but of citizens who must be reformed, educated, informed as well as entertained—in short, 'served'—presumably to enable them to better perform their democratic rights and duties. (pp. 28–29)

The effects model of the audience has been used to preserve unique radio station formats that would otherwise have fallen victim to the marketplace

(*Citizens Committee to Save WEFM v. FCC*, 1974). It lies at the heart of arguments sustaining the constitutionality of the old *Fairness Doctrine* (*Red Lion Broadcasting Co., Inc. v. FCC*, 1969), and rationalizes policies that give preferences to media owners based on their race (*Metro Broadcasting, Inc. v. Federal Communications Commission*, 1990). More generally, it appears to sustain public service broadcasting here and around the world.

The Marketplace Model

Standing in sharp contrast to the effects model is yet another vision of the mass audience that may be the most influential of all in American media policy. Rather than casting people in the role of passive victims, it portrays them as active consumers who are capable of choosing media to suit their own needs and desires. Not unlike the effects model, the marketplace model draws support from a broad intellectual base. It is buttressed by a powerful body of neoclassical economic theory (e.g., Owen & Wildman, 1992), but seems to appeal to common sense as well. Under the marketplace model, the public interest is best served by creating a media system that is fully responsive to audience preferences.

This way of thinking about the mass audience helped justify the deregulation of American media that began in the 1970s. It was stated most bluntly by Ronald Reagan's chairman of the FCC who, in direct contradiction of his predecessor, proclaimed "the public's interest ... defines the public interest" (Fowler & Brenner, 1982, p. 210). Some version of the marketplace model probably helps rationalize the trend toward the privatization of mass media in many countries around the world (Blumler, 1992).

Although the mix of U.S. print media had long been a function of market forces, as we have seen, broadcasters face special expectations as the trustees of public airwaves. One of the first broadcast policies to fall victim to an increasing reliance on the marketplace was the body of law that protected unique radio station formats from extinction. In a 1976 ruling, the FCC overturned the existing policy and declared,

> the marketplace is the best way to allocate entertainment formats in radio, whether the hoped for result is expressed in First Amendment terms (i.e., promoting the greatest diversity of listening choices for the public) or in economic terms (i.e., maximizing the welfare of consumers of radio programs). (Federal Communications Commission, 1976, p. 863)

Under the marketplace model, the audience is sovereign. If it demands diverse media materials, these will be provided in an appropriate form. If there is no demand, even for the most meritorious of content, so be it. More importantly, in the context of this discussion, the audience is only heard *en masse*. Consumer demand is recognized almost exclusively in the aggregate. In fact, the very concept of maximizing consumer welfare depends on a kind of vote counting to determine how well the system delivers preferred content to most of the people most of the time.

At the start of this discussion, we noted that models of the audience are not always easily discernible, either to the policymakers who invoke them or to the scholars who study them. In fact, it has been surprisingly easy for policymakers to defer any final judgment on the nature of the audience. The old media environment, with its structural inability to fully respond to audience demand, seems partly responsible for this ambiguity. As long as the media environment was somehow deficient, viewers could not be entirely to blame for their choices. Even Minow (1978) was reluctant to fault the audience for its "steady diet of ice cream" (p. 286). Instead, he concluded that "most of television's problems stem from a lack of competition . . . with more channels on the air, we will be able to provide every community with enough stations to offer service to all parts of the public" (p. 290).

It seems to us that the time for finessing the audience question is near an end. The old media environment is changing. The capacity of the delivery systems has expanded, and along with it has come the potential for more diverse media offerings. It is also increasingly possible for people to express the intensity of their desires by making direct payments to the media. These changes will reveal more about the nature of the audience than we are used to seeing. As this happens, we believe people will have to take a position on the audience, making it a more salient feature of the policy-making process.

Consider, for example, what happens to the effects model in the new media environment. We suspect there will be continued efforts to protect the public from harmful content (e.g., Minow & Lamay, 1995). In fact, the new media environment is likely to increase the amount of what is, arguably, injurious (e.g., indecency, violence, sexually explicit material, infomercials making deceptive claims, etc.). At the same time, technology will provide us with powerful tools to label and screen out entire categories of content. Who will make these decisions, and on what basis? Surely this exercise will require a more fully elaborated view of the audience.

Even more troublesome will be the policies that try to mitigate harm by promoting exposure to worthwhile content. If, as so many people hope, the new media environment provides a genuinely diverse set of offerings, then policies requiring diversity would seem unnecessary. If, on the other hand, there is insufficient demand for good content, then none will be forthcoming. There is reason to believe that this will happen. Entman (1989), for instance, argued that the audience is unlikely to demand adequate coverage about politics, "the unsophisticated mass audience demands or accepts current news formats, or in many cases wants no news at all; the dearth of informative 'accountability news' perpetuates an unsophisticated audience" (p. 18). Generally, it would seem that unpopular ideas or modes of expression will, by their very nature, be undersupplied by the marketplace.

Assuming that this happens, policymakers are faced with the unenviable task of trying to remedy the situation in a meaningful way. Subsidizing or requiring good programming in the old media environment might have enforced a modicum of exposure. But, with a large number of channels all competing for audience, there is a distinct possibility that no one would watch the programming that the bureaucracy has judged to be meritorious. Politically, it would be extremely difficult to mandate media content for which there is no audience. It may be that the audience will indeed be sovereign—whether we like it or not.

If the new media environment raises fundamental questions about the applicability of the effects model, it would appear to enhance the utility of the marketplace model. This is, after all, the kind of environment for which the traditional laws of supply and demand seem ideally suited. If anything, we might see greater deference paid to consumer choices in a world where sellers of content are free to enter the market and buyers can express their desires in the prices they pay for media offerings.

The principal challenge to the marketplace model is not whether it can effectively rationalize economic choices, but the extent to which it is compatible with the *marketplace of ideas*. This is one of the most powerful metaphors in communications policy (Entman & Wildman, 1992). Essentially, it stipulates that all who wish to speak should be free to do so without restraint. In theory, this provides a mechanism for discovering truth and promoting social cohesion. Some economists are inclined to argue that the economic marketplace and the marketplace of ideas are one and the same. Owen (1975), for instance, wrote:

> This very freedom to enter the market, to test consumer response, which is guaranteed by the competitive mechanism, may be all that is essential to freedom of expression (from a constitutional viewpoint) provided consumers demand the right information about political matters. Surely the framers of the constitution did not have in mind an absolute right to survival in the marketplace for all potential purveyors of ideas. (p. 27)

But even if the economic marketplace satisfies a broad range of consumer demand, producing a diverse menu from which all are free to choose, it may fail to serve the marketplace of ideas in a rather profound way.

This failure derives not from what is available in the marketplace, but how the audience copes with diversity. As Webster and Phalen (1994) point out, diversity of supply does not guarantee diversity of consumption:

Quite the contrary, as the menu of content becomes increasingly diverse, each individual is in a position to consume an ever narrower diet of programming. In fact, much of what we know about human psychology and audience behavior suggests that this is precisely how "rational" people are likely to deal with diversity. If increasing diversity of content means that each individual is actually exposed to less diversity of expression, it's hard to see how such a result facilitates the marketplace of ideas. (p. 35)

Unfortunately, this prospect is consistent with the phenomenon of audience polarization we reviewed in chapter 7. The structural features of the new media environment—the correlation of content and channels, and the differential availability of those channels—could be expected to exacerbate the tendency of individuals or subcultures to consume relatively narrow regimens of content. In effect, a new media environment that qualifies as more diverse could create audiences that rarely, if ever, experience diversity. Furthermore, for those with an activist bent, the new media environment that makes this behavior possible also undermines the basis on which government might take corrective actions.

Traditionally, American courts have relied on the existence of *spectrum scarcity* to justify regulations that imposed certain standards of fairness and balance on broadcasters. This was true even though the old media's economic motivations led them to the present broad, socially acceptable programming anyway. The new media environment, with its profusion of channels, appears to be largely immune from content regulations. If balance and diversity are to be imposed on a new media channel, then some alternative regulatory standard would have to be developed.

Schmidt (1978) raised the possibility that such a new standard could be framed in terms of audience behavior. Anticipating the possibility of extreme levels of audience polarization, Schmidt suggested that a "scarcity of viewer preferences and habit" might be used to justify government regulation (p. 215). Addressing the same problem in a somewhat more affirmative manner, Entman (1991) argued for supplementing a person's right to speak or hear with a "right to be exposed to diverse ideas" (p. 2). Although it is hard for us to imagine just how such standards of government intervention might be operationalized, either would place audience behavior at the heart of communications policy.

These issues are likely to present a growing quandary for students of media and society. We noted in chapter 2 that the communications discipline has become enamored of an active model of the audience—individuals freely making choices and meanings (Bryant & Street, 1988). This is certainly an appealing way to conceive of people, as it affords them a measure of rationality and power. Yet, when we set these active individuals loose in the world of media, as the marketplace model would have us do, the net result can often be disappointing. Does that mean that, in the aggregate, active individuals have been transformed into a passive mass needing government protection? The mass audience concept, with its ability to accommodate notions of activity (e.g., individuals choosing preferred content), while still recognizing the power of structural factors to determine exposure may provide a way to reason through the quandary.

Likewise, mass audience thinking has much to offer the field of media studies. So many of our disciplinary concerns seem to begin after the reader engages the text, be it radio, television, magazines or movies. We ask, in one way or another, how the text resonates with audience experience. Does the film position the viewer in such a way that only preferred readings are possible? What role do people have in making meaning from the media? What are the uses and pleasures of watching television? What are the effects of exposure to media messages? These are certainly significant questions that have engaged researchers for several decades. But, they are often asked to the exclusion of what strikes us as an increasingly important set of questions.

How is it that large numbers of people come into contact with the text in the first place? What does that tell us about the consumption of popular culture? Can media create or sustain various publics? How might the formation of audiences circumscribe or extend the power of the media to shape our society? Simple notions of audience activity do not adequately answer these questions. It is here that the mass audience concept can be of considerable value. It reveals much to those who recognize its flexibility and study it with imagination. It is time to rediscover the dominant model.

References*

Adams, W. J., Eastman, S. T., Horney, L. J., & Popovich, M. N. (1983). The cancellation and manipulation of network television prime-time programs. *Journal of Communication, 33(1)*, 10–27.

Agostini, J. M. (1961). How to estimate unduplicated audiences. *Journal of Advertising Research, 1*, 11–14.

Agostino, D. (1980). Cable television's impact on the audience of public television. *Journal of Broadcasting, 24*, 347–363.

Allen, C. (1965). Photographing the TV audience. *Journal of Advertising Research, 5*, 2–8.

Allen, R. (1981). The reliability and stability of television exposure. *Communication Research, 8*, 233–256.

Anderson, B. (1991). *Imagined communities* (Rev Ed.). London: Verso.

Anderson, D. R., & Lorch, E. P. (1983). Looking at television: Action or reaction? In J. Bryant & D. Anderson (Eds.), *Children's understanding of television* (pp. 1–33). New York: Academic Press.

Anderson, J. A., & Meyer, T. P. (1988). *Mediated communication: A social action perspective.* Newbury Park, CA: Sage.

Ang, I. (1989). Wanted: Audiences. On the politics of empirical audience studies. In E. Seiter, H. Borchers, G. Kreutzner, & E. Warth (Eds.), *Remote control: Television, audiences & cultural power* (pp. 96–115). London: Routledge.

Ang, I. (1991). *Desperately seeking the audience.* London: Routledge.

Aske Research Ltd. (1978). *Availability to view* [Report prepared for the Independent Broadcasting Authority]. London: Author.

Aske Research Ltd. (1980). *The effort of switching channels.* [Report prepared for the Independent Broadcasting Authority]. London: Author.

Atkin, D., & Litman, B. (1986). Network TV programming: Economics, audiences, and the ratings game, 1971–1986. *Journal of Communication, 36(3)*, 32–51.

Austin, B. A. (1989)., *Immediate seating: A look at movie audiences.* Belmont, CA: Wadsworth.

Babrow, A. S., & Swanson, D. L. (1988). Disentangling antecedents of audience exposure levels: Extending expectancy-value analyses of gratifications sought from television news. *Communication Monographs, 55*, 1–21.

Bagdikian, B. H. (1985). The U. S. media: Supermarket or assembly line? *Journal of Communication, 35(3)*, 97–109.

Bagdikian, B. H. (1992). *The media monopoly* (4th ed.). Boston: Beacon Press.

---

*This reference section includes all works cited in the text, as well as other relevant readings.

Baldwin, T. F., Barnett, M., & Bates, B., (1992). Influence of cable on television news audiences. *Journalism Quarterly, 69*, 651–658.

Banks, M. (1981). *A history of broadcast audience research in the United States, 1920–1980 with an emphasis on the rating services.* Unpublished doctoral dissertation, University of Tennessee, Knoxville, TN.

Banning, W. P. (1946). *Commercial broadcasting pioneer: The WEAF experiment 1922–1926.* Cambridge: Harvard University Press.

Barnes, B. E. (1990). *Electronic media audience behavior in the multichannel environment: Patterns of demographic homogeneity and time spent viewing.* Unpublished doctoral dissertation, Northwestern University, Evanston, IL.

Barnes, B. E., & Thomson, L. M. (1994). Power to the people (meter): Audience measurement technology and media specialization. In J. Ettema & D.C. Whitney (Eds.), *Audiencemaking: How the media create the audience* (pp. 75–94). Thousand Oaks, CA: Sage.

Barnett, G. A., Chang, H., Fink, E. L., & Richards, W. D. (1991). Seasonality in television viewing: A mathematical model of cultural processes. *Communication Research, 18*(6), 755–772.

Barwise, T. P. (1986). Repeat-viewing of prime-time television series. *Journal of Advertising Research, 26,* 9–14.

Barwise, T. P., & Ehrenberg, A. S. C. (1984). The reach of TV channels. *International Journal of Research in Marketing, 1,* 34–49.

Barwise, T. P., & Ehrenberg, A. S. C. (1988). *Television and its audience.* London: Sage.

Barwise, T. P., Ehrenberg, A. S. C., & Goodhardt, G. J. (1979). Audience appreciation and audience size. *Journal of the Market Research Society, 21,* 269–289.

Barwise, T. P., Ehrenberg, A. S. C., & Goodhardt, G. J. (1982). Glued to the box?: Patterns of TV repeat-viewing. *Journal of Communication, 32*(4), 22–29.

Bauer, C. L., & Fink, E. L. (1983). Fitting equations with power transformations: Examining variables with error. In R. N. Bostrom (Ed.), *Communication Yearbook 7* (pp. 146–199). Beverly Hills, CA: Sage.

Bechtel, R. K., Achelpohl, C., & Akers, R. (1972). Correlation between observed behavior and questionnaire responses on television viewing. In E. A. Rubinstein, G. A. Comstock, & J. P. Murray (Eds.), *Television and social behavior: Vol. 4. Television in day-to-day life: Patterns of use* (pp. 274–344). Washington, DC: U.S. Government Printing Office.

Becker, L. B., & Schoenback, K. (Eds.). (1989). *Audience responses to media diversification: Coping with plenty.* Hillsdale, NJ: Lawrence Erlbaum Associates.

Beebe, J. H. (1977). The institutional structure and program choices in television markets. *Quarterly Journal of Economics, 91,* 15–37.

Beniger, J. R. (1986). *The control revolution: Technological and economic origins of the information society.* Cambridge, MA: Harvard University Press.

Beniger, J. R. (1987). Toward an old new paradigm: The half-century flirtation with mass society. *Public Opinion Quarterly, 51* (Suppl.), S46–S66.

Besen, S. M. (1976). The value of television time. *Southern Economic Journal, 42,* 435–441.

Besen, S. M., Krattenmaker, T. G., Metzger, A. R., & Woodbury, J. R. (1984). *Misregulating television: Network dominance and the FCC.* Chicago: University of Chicago Press.

Besen, S. M., & Mitchell, B. M. (1976). Watergate and television: An economic analysis. *Communication Research, 3,* 243–260.

Beville, H. M., Jr. (1988). *Audience ratings: Radio, television, cable* (rev. ed.). Hillsdale, NJ: Lawrence Erlbaum Associates.

Black, J., & Bryant, J. (1995). *Introduction to media communication* (4th ed.). Dubuque, IA: Brown and Benchmark.

Blumer, H. (1946). The field of collective behavior. In A. M. Lee (Ed.), *New outline of the principles of sociology* (pp. 167–222). New York: Barnes & Noble.

Blumler, J. G. (1979). The role of theory in uses and gratifications studies. *Communication Research, 6,* 9–36.

Blumler, J. G. (Ed.). (1992). *Television and the public interest: Vulnerable values in West European broadcasting.* London: Sage.

Blumler, J. G., Gurevitch, M., & Katz, E. (1985). Reaching out: A future for gratifications research. In K. Rosengren, L. Wenner, & P. Palmgreen (Eds.), *Media gratifications research: Current perspectives* (pp. 255–273). Beverly Hills, CA: Sage.

Boemer, M. L. (1987). Correlating lead-in show ratings with local television news ratings. *Journal of Broadcasting & Electronic Media, 31,* 89–94.

Bogart, L. (1972). *The age of television.* New York: Ungar.

Bourdieu, P. (1984). *Distinction: A critique of the judgement of taste.* Cambridge, MA: Harvard University Press.

Bower, R. T. (1973). *Television and the public.* New York: Holt, Rinehart & Winston.

Bower, R. T. (1985). *The changing television audience in America.* New York: Columbia University Press.

Bowman, G. W., & Farley, J. (1972). TV viewing: Application of a formal choice model. *Applied Economics, 4,* 245–259.

Brockett, O. G. (1968). *History of the Theatre.* Boston: Allyn and Bacon.

Brosius, H. B., Wober, M., & Weimann, G. (1992). The loyalty of television viewing: How consistent is TV viewing behavior? *Journal of Broadcasting & Electronic Media, 36,* 321–335.

Bruno, A. V. (1973). The network factor in TV viewing. *Journal of Advertising Research, 13,* 33–39.

Bryant, J., & Street, R. L. (1988). From reactivity to activity and action: An evolving concept and weltanschauung in mass and interpersonal communication. In R. Hawkins, J. Wiemann, & S. Pingree (Eds.), *Advancing communication science: Merging mass and interpersonal processes,* (pp.162–190). Newbury Park, CA: Sage.

Bryant, J., & Zillmann, D. (1984). Using television to alleviate boredom and stress: Selective exposure as a function of induced excitational states. *Journal of Broadcasting, 28,* 1–20.

Bryant, J., & Zillmann, D., (Eds.). (1986). *Perspectives on media effects.* Hillsdale, NJ: Lawrence Erlbaum Associates.

Bryant, J., & Zillmann, D., (Eds.). (1994). *Media effects: Advances in theory and research.* Hillsdale, NJ: Lawrence Erlbaum Associates.

Butler v. Michigan, 352 U.S. 380 (1957).

Buzzard, K. S. (1990). *Chains of gold: Marketing the ratings and rating the markets.* Metuchen, NJ: Scarecrow Press.

Cabletelevision Advertising Bureau. (1995). *Cable TV facts.* New York: Author.

Cannon, H. M. (1983). Reach and frequency estimates for specialized target markets. *Journal of Advertising Research, 23,* 45–50.

Cannon, H., & Merz, G. R. (1980). A new role for psychographics in media selection. *Journal of Advertising, 9*(2), 33–36.

Cantor, M. G. (1994). The role of audience in the production of culture: A personal research retrospective. In J. Ettema & D.C. Whitney (Eds.), *Audiencemaking: How the media create the audience* (pp. 159–170). Thousand Oaks, CA: Sage.

Cantor, M. G., & Cantor, J. M. (1986). Audience composition and television content: The mass audience revisited. In S. Ball-Rokeach & M. Cantor (Eds.), *Media, audience, and social structure* (pp. 214–225). Newbury Park, CA: Sage.

Cantril, H., & Allport, G. W. (1935). *The psychology of radio.* New York: Harper & Brothers.

Carey, J., & Kreiling, A. L. (1974). Popular culture and uses and gratifications: Notes toward an accommodation. In J. Blumler & E. Katz (Eds.), *The uses of mass communications* (pp. 225–248). Beverly Hills, CA: Sage.

Carroll Broadcasting Company v. FCC, 258 F. 440 (1958).

Chaffee, S. (1980). Mass media effects: New research perspectives. In D. C. Wilhoit & H. DeBock (Eds.), *Mass communication review yearbook* (pp. 77–108). Beverly Hills, CA: Sage.

Chaffee, S. & Hochheimer, J. (1985). The beginnings of political communication research in the United States: Origins of the "limited effects" model. In M. Gurevitch & M. R. Levy (Eds.), *Mass communication review yearbook* (pp. 75–104). Beverly Hills, CA: Sage.

Chandon, J. L. (1976). *A comparative study of media exposure models.* Unpublished doctoral dissertation, Northwestern University, Evanston, IL.

Chappell, M. N., & Hooper, C. E. (1944). *Radio audience measurement.* New York: Stephen Daye.

Christ, W., & Medoff, N. (1984). Affective state and selective exposure to and use of television. *Journal of Broadcasting, 28,* 51–63.

Christenson, E. G., & Peterson, J. B. (1988). Genre and gender in the structure of music preferences. *Communication Research, 15*(3), 282–301.

Citizens Committee to Save WEFM v. FCC, 506 F. 246 (1974).

Cohen, E. E. (1989). *A model of radio listener choice.* Unpublished doctoral dissertation, Michigan State University, East Lansing, MI.

Collins, J., Reagan, J., & Abel, J. (1983). Predicting cable subscribership: Local factors. *Journal of Broadcasting, 27,* 177–183.

Comstock, G. (1980). *Television in America.* Beverly Hills, CA: Sage.

Comstock, G. (1989). *The evolution of American television.* Newbury Park, CA: Sage.

Comstock, G., Chaffee, S., Katzman, N., McCombs, M., & Roberts, D. (1978). *Television and human behavior.* New York: Columbia University Press.

Cook, T. D., Kendzierski, D. A., & Thomas, S. V. (1983). The implicit assumptions of television research: An analysis of the 1982 NIMH report on television and behavior. *Public Opinion Quarterly, 47,* 161–201.

Cooper, R. (1993). An expanded, integrated model for determining audience exposure to television. *Journal of Broadcasting & Electronic Media, 37,* 401–418.

Cooper, R. (1996). The status and future of audience duplication research: An assessment of ratings-based theories of audience behavior. *Journal of Broadcasting & Electronic Media, 40,* 96–111.

Cotton, J. L. (1985). Cognitive dissonance in selective exposure. In D. Zillmann & J. Bryant (Eds.), *Selective exposure to communication* (pp. 11–33). Hillsdale, NJ: Lawrence Erlbaum Associates.

Csikszentmihalyi, M., & Kubey, R. (1981). Television and the rest of life: A systematic comparison of subjective experience. *Public Opinion Quarterly, 45,* 317–328.

Czitrom, D. J. (1982). *Media and the American mind: From Morse to McLuhan.* Chapel Hill, NC: University of North Carolina Press.

Darmon, R. (1976). Determinants of TV viewing. *Journal of Advertising Research, 16,* 17–20.

Davison, W. P. (1983). The third person effect in communication. *Public Opinion Quarterly, 47,* 1–15.

Dayan, D., & Katz, E. (1992). *Media events: The live broadcasting of history.* Cambridge, MA: Harvard University Press.

DeFleur, M. L. & Ball-Rokeach, S. (1982). *Theories of mass communication* (4th ed.). New York: Longman.

Dizard, W. (1994). *Old media/New media: Mass communications in the information age.* New York: Longman.

Dobrow, J. R. (1989). Away from the mainstream? VCR's and ethnic identity. In M. Levy (Ed.), *The VCR age: Home video and mass communication* (pp. 193–208). Newbury Park, CA: Sage.

Dobrow, J. R. (1990). *Social and cultural aspects of VCR use.* Hillsdale, NJ: Lawrence Erlbaum Associates.

Ducey, R., Krugman, D., & Eckrich, D. (1983). Predicting market segments in the cable industry: The basic and pay subscribers. *Journal of Broadcasting, 27,* 155–161.

Eastman, S. T. (Ed.). (1993). *Broadcast/cable programming: Strategies and practices* (4th ed). Belmont, CA: Wadsworth.

Eastman, S. T., & Newton, G. D. (1995). Delineating grazing: Observations of remote control use. *Journal of Communication, 45*(1), 77–95.

Ehrenberg, A. S. C. (1968). The factor analytic search for program types. *Journal of Advertising Research, 8,* 55–63.

Ehrenberg, A. S. C. (1986, February). Advertisers or viewers paying? *ADMAP Monograph.*

Ehrenberg, A. S. C., & Wakshlag, J. (1987). Repeat-viewing with people meters. *Journal of Advertising Research, 27,* 9–13.

Ehrenberg, A. S. C., Goodhardt, G. J., & Barwise, T. P. (1990). Double jeopardy revisited. *Journal of Marketing, 54,* 82–91.

Elliot, P. (1974). Uses and gratifications research: A critique and a sociological alternative. In J.G. Blumler & E. Katz (Eds.), *The uses of mass communications: Current perspectives on gratifications research* (pp. 249–268). Beverly Hills, CA: Sage.

Ellis, J. (1983). Channel 4: Working notes. *Screen, 24,* 37–51.

Entman, R. M. (1989). *Democracy without citizens: Media and the decay of American politics.* New York: Oxford University Press.

Entman, R. M., (April, 1991). *A policy analytical approach to the First Amendment.* Paper presented at the 1991 Research Conference for the Bicentennial of the First Amendment, Williamsburg, VA.

Entman, R. M., & Wildman, S. S. (1992). Reconciling economic and non-economic perspectives on media policy: Transcending the "Marketplace of Ideas." *Journal of Communication, 42*(1), 5–19.

Escarpit, R. (1977). The concept of "mass." *Journal of Communication 27*(2), 44–48.

Ettema, J. S., & Whitney, D. C., (Eds.). (1982). *Individuals in mass media organizations: Creativity and constraint.* Beverly Hills, CA: Sage.

Ettema, J. S. & Whitney, D. C. (1994). The money arrow: An introduction to audiencemaking. In J. Ettema & D. C. Whitney (Eds.), *Audiencemaking: How the media create the audience* (pp. 1–18). Thousand Oaks, CA: Sage.

Federal Communications Commission. (1976). *In the matter of development of policy re: changes in entertainment formats for broadcast stations,* 60 F.C.C. 858.

Federal Radio Commission. (1928). *Statement made by the Commission, August 23, 1928, relative to public interest, convenience, or necessity,* 2 F.R.C. Ann. Rep. 166.

Fejes, F. (1984). Critical mass communications research and media effects: The problem of the disappearing audience. *Media, Culture and Society, 6,* 219–232.

Ferguson, D. A. (1994). Measurement of mundane TV behaviors: Remote control device flipping frequency. *Journal of Broadcasting and Electronic Media, 38*(1), 35–47.

Ferguson, D. A., & Perse, E. M. (1993). Media and audience influences on channel repertoire. *Journal of Broadcasting and Electronic Media, 37*(1), 31–47.

Festinger, L. (1957). *A theory of cognitive dissonance.* Evanston, IL: Row, Peterson.

Fink, E., Robinson, J., & Dowden, S. (1985). The structure of music preference and attendance. *Communication Research, 12*(3), 301–318.

Fisher, F. M., McGowan, J. J., & Evans, D. S. (1980). The audience-revenue relationship for local television stations. *Bell Journal of Economics, 11,* 694–708.

Fletcher, J. E. (Ed.). (1981). *Handbook of radio and TV broadcasting: Research procedures in audience, program and revenues.* New York: Van Nostrand Reinhold.

Foote, J. S. (1988). Ratings decline of presidential television. *Journal of Broadcasting and Electronic Media, 32,* 225–230.

Foucault, M. (1977). *Discipline and Punish: The birth of the prison.* (Alan Sheridan, Trans.). New York: Vintage.

Fournier, G. M., & Martin, D. L. (1983). Does government-restricted entry produce market power? New evidence from the market for television advertising. *Bell Journal of Economics, 14*, 44–56.

Fowler, M. S., & Brenner, D. L. (1982). A marketplace approach to broadcast regulation. *Texas Law Review, 60*, 207–257.

Frank, R. E., Becknell, J., & Clokey, J. (1971). Television program types. *Journal of Marketing Research, 11*, 204–211.

Frank, R. E., & Greenberg, M. G. (1980). *The public's use of television.* Beverly Hills, CA: Sage.

Fratrik, M. R. (1989, April). *The television audience-revenue relationship revisited.* Paper presented at the meeting of the Broadcast Education Association, Las Vegas, NV.

Freidson, E. (1953). Communications research and the concept of the mass. *American Sociological Review, 18*, 313–317.

Galbraith, J. K. (1967). *The new industrial state.* (3rd rev. ed.). Boston: Houghton Mifflin.

Gandy, O. H. (1992). The political economy approach: A critical challenge. *Journal of Media Economics, 5*, 23–42.

Gandy, O. H. (1993). *The panoptic sort: A political economy of personal information.* Boulder, CO: Westview.

Gans, H. (1974). *Popular culture and high culture: An analysis and evaluation of taste.* New York: Basic Books.

Gans, H. (1980). The audience for television—and in television research. In S. B. Witney & R. P. Abeles (Eds.), *Television and social behavior: Beyond violence and children* (pp. 55–81). Hillsdale, NJ: Lawrence Erlbaum Associates.

Gantz, W., & Eastman, S. T. (1983). Viewer uses of promotional media to find out about television programs. *Journal of Broadcasting, 27*, 269–277.

Gantz, W., & Razazahoori, A. (1982). The impact of television schedule changes on audience viewing behaviors. *Journalism Quarterly, 59*, 265–272.

Gensch, D. H., & Ranganathan, B. (1974). Evaluation of television program content for the purpose of promotional segmentation. *Journal of Marketing Research, 11*, 390–398.

Gensch, D. H., & Shaman, P. (1980). Models of competitive ratings. *Journal of Marketing Research, 17*, 307–315.

Gerbner, G., & Gross, L. (1976). Living with television: The violence profile. *Journal of Communication, 26*, 173–199.

Gerbner, G., Gross, L., Morgan, M., & Signorielli, N. (1984). Political correlates of television viewing. *Public Opinion Quarterly, 48*, 283–300.

Gerbner, G., Gross, L., Morgan, M., & Signorielli, N. (1986). Living with television: The dynamics of the cultivation process. In J. Bryant & D. Zillmann (Eds.), *Perspectives on media effects* (pp. 17–40). Hillsdale, NJ: Lawrence Erlbaum Associates.

Gitlin, T. (1978). Media sociology: The dominant paradigm. *Theory and Society, 6*, 205–253.

Gitlin, T. (1983). *Inside prime time.* New York: Pantheon.

Gomery, D. (1993). The contemporary American movie business. In A. Alexander, J. Owers, & R. Carveth (Eds.), *Media economics: Theory and practice* (pp. 267–282). Hillsdale, NJ: Lawrence Erlbaum Associates.

Goodhardt, G. J. (1966). The constant in duplicated television viewing between and within channels. *Nature, 212*, 1616.

Goodhardt, G. J., & Ehrenberg, A. S. C. (1969). Duplication of viewing between and within channels. *Journal of Marketing Research, 6*, 169–178.

Goodhardt, G. J., Ehrenberg, A. S. C., & Collins, M. A. (1975). *The television audience: Patterns of viewing.* Westmead, UK: Saxon House.

Goodhardt, G. J., Ehrenberg, A. S. C., & Collins, M. A. (1987). *The television audience: Patterns of viewing* (2nd ed.). Westmead, UK: Gower.

Grant, A. E. (1989). *Exploring patterns of television viewing: A media system dependency perspective.* Unpublished doctoral dissertation, University of Southern California, Los Angeles, CA.

Greenberg, E., & Barnett, H. J. (1971). TV program diversity—New evidence and old theories. *American Economic Review, 61,* 89–93.

Greenberg, B., Dervin, B., & Dominick, J. (1968). Do people watch 'television' or 'programs'?: A measurement problem. *Journal of Broadcasting, 12,* 367–376.

Haldi, J. A. (1981). Network affiliate programming. In S. T. Eastman, S. W. Head, & L. Klein (Eds.), *Broadcast programming: Strategies for winning television and radio audiences* (pp. 89–106). Belmont, CA: Wadsworth.

Hall, S. (1980). Encoding/decoding. In S. Hall, D. Hobson, A. Lowe, & P. Willis (Eds.), *Culture, media, language.* (pp. 197–208) London: Hutchinson.

Head, S., & Sterling, C. (1987). *Broadcasting in America* (5th ed.). Boston: Houghton Mifflin Company.

Headen, R. S., Klompmaker, J., & Rust, R. (1979). The duplication of viewing law and television media schedule evaluation. *Journal of Marketing Research, 16,* 333–340.

Headen, R. S., Klompmaker, J. E., & Teel, J. E. (1977). Predicting audience exposure to spot TV advertising schedules. *Journal of Marketing Research, 14,* 1–9.

Headen, R. S., Klompmaker, J. E., & Teel, J. E. (1979). Predicting network TV viewing patterns. *Journal of Advertising Research, 19,* 49–54.

Hearn, G. (1989). Active and passive conceptions of the television audience: Effects of a change in viewing routine. *Human Relations, 42*(10), 857–875.

Heeter, C. (1988). The choice process model. In C. Heeter & B. Greenberg (Eds.), *Cable-viewing* (pp. 11–32). Norwood, NJ: Ablex.

Heeter, C., & Greenberg, B. S. (1985). Cable and program choice. In D. Zillmann & J. Bryant (Eds.), *Selective exposure to communication* (pp. 203–224). Hillsdale, NJ: Lawrence Erlbaum Associates.

Heeter, C., & Greenberg, B. S. (1985). Profiling the zappers. *Journal of Advertising Research, 25*(2), 15–19.

Heeter, C., & Greenberg, B. S. (1988). *Cable-viewing.* Norwood, NJ: Ablex.

Henriksen, F. (1985). A new model of the duplication of television viewing: A behaviorist approach. *Journal of Broadcasting & Electronic Media, 29,* 135–145.

Herbst, S. (1993). *Numbered voices: How opinion polling has shaped American politics.* Chicago: University of Chicago Press.

Herbst, S. & Beniger, J. R. (1994). The changing infrastructure of public opinion. In J. Ettema & D. C. Whitney (Eds.), *Audiencemaking: How the media create the audience* (pp. 95–114). Thousand Oaks, CA: Sage.

Herzog, H. (1944). What do we really know about daytime serial listeners? In P. F. Lazersfeld & F. N. Stanton (Eds.), *Radio research 1942–1943* (pp. 23–36). New York: Duell, Sloan & Pearce.

Hill, D., & Dyer, J. (1981). Extent of diversion to newscasts from distant stations by cable viewers. *Journalism Quarterly, 58,* 552–555.

Hirsch, P. (1980). An organizational perspective on television (Aided and abetted by models from economics, marketing, and the humanities). In S. B. Withey & R. P. Abeles (Eds.), *Television and social behavior* (pp. 83–102). Hillsdale, NJ: Lawrence Erlbaum Associates.

Hirsch, P. (1982). The role of television and popular culture in contemporary society. In H. Newcomb (Ed.), *Television: The critical view* (3rd ed., pp. 280–310). New York: Oxford University Press.

Hogarth, R. M., & Reder, M. W., (Eds.). (1986). *Rational choice: The contrast between economics and psychology.* Chicago: University of Chicago Press.

Horen, J. H. (1980). Scheduling of network television programs. *Management Science, 26,* 354–370.

Hotelling, H. (1929). Stability in competition. *Economic Journal, 34,* 41–57.

Hurwitz, D. L. (1983). *Broadcast "ratings": The rise and development of commercial audience research and measurement in American broadcasting.* Unpublished doctoral dissertation, University of Illinois, Urbana, IL.

Israel, H., & Robinson, J. (1972). Demographic characteristics of viewers of television violence and news programs. In E. A. Rubinstein, G. A. Comstock, & J. P. Murray (Eds.), *Television and social behavior: Vol. 4. Television in day-to-day life: Patterns of use* (pp. 87–128). Washington, DC: U.S. Government Printing Office.

Jacobs, R. (1995). Exploring the determinants of cable television subscriber satisfaction. *Journal of Broadcasting & Electronic Media, 39,* 262–274.

Jeffres, L. W. (1978). Cable TV and viewer selectivity. *Journal of Broadcasting, 22,* 167–177.

Jeffres, L. W. (1986). *Mass media processes and effects.* Prospect Heights, IL: Waveland.

Jensen, K. B. (1987). Qualitative audience research: Toward an integrative approach to reception. *Critical Studies in Mass Communication, 4,* 21–36.

Jensen, K. B., & Rosengren, K. E. (1990). Five traditions in search of the audience. *European Journal of Communication, 5,* 207–238.

Jhally, S., & Livant, B. (1986). Watching as working: The valorization of audience consciousness. *Journal of Communication, 36*(3), 124–143.

Katz, E. (1983) Publicity and pluralistic ignorance: Notes on the "spiral of silence." In E. Wartella & D. C. Whitney (Eds.), *Mass communication review yearbook* (Vol. 4, pp. 89–99). Beverly Hills, CA: Sage.

Katz, E. (1987). Communication research since Lazarsfeld. *Public Opinion Quarterly, 51* (Suppl.), S25–S45.

Katz, E., Blumler, J. G., & Gurevitch, M. (1974). Utilization of mass communication by the individual. In J. G. Blumler & E. Katz (Eds.), *The uses of mass communications: Current perspectives on gratifications research* (pp. 19–32). Beverly Hills, CA: Sage.

Katz, E., Gurevitch, M., & Haas, H. (1973). On the use of mass media for important things. *American Sociological Review, 38*(2), 164–181.

Katz, E., & Lazarsfeld, P. F. (1955). *Personal influence: The part played by people in the flow of mass communications.* Glencoe, IL: Free Press.

Kim, M. S., & Hunter, J. E. (1993). Attitude-behavior relations: A meta-analysis of attitudinal relevance and topic. *Journal of Communication, 43*(1), 101–142.

Kirsch, A. D., & Banks, S. (1962). Program types defined by factor analysis. *Journal of Advertising Research, 2,* 29–31.

Klapper, J. (1960). *The effects of mass communication.* Glencoe, IL: The Free Press.

Klein, P. (1971, January). The men who run TV aren't stupid.... *New York,* 20–29.

Krugman, D. M. (1985). Evaluating the audiences of the new media. *Journal of Advertising, 14*(4), 21–27.

Kubey, R., & Csikszentmihalyi, M. (1990). *Television and the quality of life: How viewing shapes everyday experience.* Hillsdale, NJ: Lawrence Erlbaum Associates.

Kubey, R., Shifflet, M., Weerakkody, N., & Ukeiley, S. (1995). Demographic diversity on cable: Have the new cable channels made a difference in the representation of gender, race, and age? *Journal of Broadcasting & Electronic Media, 39,* 459–471.

LaRose, R., & Atkin, D. (1988). Satisfaction, demographic, and media environment predictors of cable subscription. *Journal of Broadcasting & Electronic Media, 32,* 403–413.

Larson, E. (1992). *The naked consumer: How our private lives become public commodities.* New York: Henry Holt and Company.

Lasswell, H. D. (1948). The structure and function of communication in society. In W. Schramm & D. Roberts (Eds.), *The process and effects of mass communication* (rev. ed., pp. 84–99). Urbana: University of Illinois Press.

Lazarsfeld, P. F. (1941). Remarks on administrative and critical communications research. *Studies of Philosophy and Social Science, 9*(1) 2–16.

Lazarsfeld, P. F. (1946). *The people look at radio.* Chapel Hill: The University of North Carolina Press.

Lazarsfeld, P. F., & Merton, R. K. (1948). Mass communication, popular taste, and organized social action. In Bryson (Ed.), *The communication of ideas* (pp. 95–118). New York: Cooper Square Publishers.

Lazarsfeld, P. F., & Stanton, F. N. (Eds.). (1941). *Radio research.* New York: Duell, Sloan & Pearce.

Lazer, W. (1987). *Handbook of demographics for marketing and advertising.* Lexington, MA: Lexington Books.

Leckenby, J. D., & Rice, M. D. (1985). A beta binomial network TV exposure model using limited data. *Journal of Advertising, 3,* 25–31.

LeDuc, D. R. (1987). *Beyond broadcasting: Patterns in policy and law.* New York: Longman.

Lehmann, D. R. (1971). Television show preference: Application of a choice model. *Journal of Marketing Research, 8,* 47–55.

Levin, H. G. (1980). *Fact and fancy in television regulation: An economic study of policy alternatives.* New York: Russell Sage.

Levy, M. R. (1978). The audience experience with television news. *Journalism Monographs, 55.*

Levy, M. R. (Ed.). (1989). *The VCR age: Home video and mass communication.* Newbury Park, CA: Sage.

Levy, M. R., & Fink, E. L. (1984). Home video recorders and the transience of television broadcasts. *Journal of Communication, 34*(2), 56–71.

Levy, M. R., & Windahl, S. (1984). Audience activity and gratifications: A conceptual clarification and exploration. *Communication Research, 11,* 51–78.

Lewis, G. (1981). Taste cultures and their composition: Towards a new theoretical perspective. In E. Katz & T. Szecsko (Eds.), *Mass media and social change* (pp. 201–217). Beverly Hills, CA: Sage.

Lichty, L., & Topping, M. (Eds.). (1975). *American broadcasting: A sourcebook on the history of radio and television.* New York: Hastings House.

Lin, C. A. (1993). Exploring the role of VCR use in the emerging home entertainment culture. *Journalism Quarterly, 70* (4), 833–842.

Lin, C. A. (1995). Network prime-time programming strategies in the 1980's. *Journal of Broadcasting & Electronic Media, 39,* 482–495.

Lindlof, T. R. (Ed.). (1987). *Natural audiences: Qualitative research on media uses and effects.* Norwood, NJ: Ablex.

Lindlof, T. R. (1991). The qualitative study of media audiences. *Journal of Broadcasting & Electronic Media, 35,* 23–42.

Litman, B. R. (1979). Predicting TV ratings for theatrical movies. *Journalism Quarterly, 56,* 591–594.

Litman, B. R., & Kohl, L. S. (1992). Network rerun viewing in the age of new programming services. *Journalism Quarterly, 69,* 383–391.

Little, J. D. C., & Lodish, L. M. (1969). A media planning calculus. *Operations Research, 1,* 1–35.

Livingstone, S. M. (1993). The rise and fall of audience research: An old story with a new ending. *Journal of Communication, 43*(4), 5–12.

LoSciuto, L. A. (1972). A national inventory of television viewing behavior. In E. A. Rubinstein, G. A. Comstock, & J. P. Murray (Eds.), *Television and social behavior: Vol. 4. Television in day-to-day life: Patterns of use* (pp. 33–86). Washington: U.S. Government Printing Office.

Lowery, S., & DeFleur, M. L. (1987). *Milestones in mass communication research: Media effects* (2nd ed.). New York: Longman.

Lull, J. (1980). The social uses of television. *Human Communication Research, 6,* 197–209.

Lull, J. (1982). How families select television programs: A mass observational study. *Journal of Broadcasting, 26,* 801–812.

Lull, J. (Ed.). (1988). *World families watch television.* Newbury Park, CA: Sage.

Lull, J. (1990). *Inside family viewing.* London: Routledge

Lumley, F. H. (1934). *Measurement in radio.* Columbus, OH: The Ohio State University.

MacFarland, D. T. (1990). *Contemporary radio programming strategies.* Hillsdale, NJ: Lawrence Erlbaum Associates.

Maisel, R. (1973). The decline of the mass media. *Public Opinion Quarterly, 37,* 159–170.

Mansfield, E. (1970). *Microeconomics: Theory and applications* (2nd ed). New York: Norton.

Marx, K., & Engels, F. (1976). *The German ideology* (3rd. ed). Moscow: Progress Publishers.

Maxwell, R. (1991). The image is gold: Value, the audience commodity, and fetishism. *Journal of Film & Video, 43,* 29–45.

McCombs, M. E., & Shaw, D. L. (1972). The agenda-setting function of the mass media. *Public Opinion Quarterly, 36,* 176–187.

McDonald, D. G., & Reese, S. D. (1987). Television news and audience selectivity. *Journalism Quarterly, 64,* 763–768.

McDonald, D. G., & Schechter, R. (1988). Audience role in the evolution of fictional television content. *Journal of Broadcasting & Electronic Media, 32,* 61–71.

McLeod, J. M., & McDonald, D. G. (1985). Beyond simple exposure: Media orientations and their impact on political processes. *Communication Research, 12,* 3–33.

McPhee, W. N. (1963). *Formal theories of mass behavior.* New York: The Free Press.

McQuail, D. (1987). *Mass communication theory: An introduction.* London: Sage.

McQuail, D. (1992). *Media performance: Mass communication and the public interest.* London: Sage.

McQuail, D. (1994). *Mass communication theory: An introduction* (3rd ed.). London: Sage.

McQuail, D., & Gurevitch, M. (1974). Explaining audience behavior: Three approaches considered. In J. G. Blumler & E. Katz (Eds.), *The uses of mass communications: Current perspectives on gratifications research* (pp. 287–302). Beverly Hills, CA: Sage.

Meehan, E. R. (1984). Ratings and the institutional approach: A third answer to the commodity question. *Critical Studies in Mass Communication, 1,* 216–225.

Meehan, E. R. (1990). Why we don't count. The commodity audience. In P. Mellencamp (Ed.), *Logics of television: Cultural criticism* (pp. 117–137). Bloomington, IN: Indiana University Press.

Meehan, E. R. (1993). Commodity audience, actual audience: The blindspot debate. In J. Wasko, V. Mosco, & M. Pendakur (Eds.), *Illuminating the blindspots: Essays honoring Dallas W. Smythe* (pp. 378–397). Norwood, NJ: Ablex.

Metro Broadcasting, Inc. v. Federal Communications Commission, 110 S. Ct. 2997 (1990).

Miller, P. V. (1994). Made-to-order and standardized audiences: Forms of reality in audience measurement. In J. S. Ettema & D. C. Whitney (Eds.), *Audiencemaking: How the media create the audience* (pp. 57–74). Thousand Oaks, CA: Sage.

Minow, N. N. (1978). Address by Newton N. Minow to the National Association of Broadcasters, Washington, DC. In F. Kahn (Ed.), *Documents of American broadcasting* (3rd ed.) (pp. 281–291). Englewood Cliffs, NJ: Prentice Hall.

Minow, N. N., & Lamay, G. L. (1995). *Abandoned in the Wasteland: Children, television, and the first amendment.* New York: Hill and Wang.

Mitchell, J., & Blumler, J. G., (Eds.). (1994). *Television and the viewer interest: Explorations in the responsiveness of European Broadcasters.* London: John Libbey.

Moores, S. (1993). *Interpreting audiences: The ethnography of media consumption.* London: Sage.

Morely, D. (1985). Cultural transformations: The politics of resistance. In M. Gurevitch & M. R. Levy (Eds.), *Mass communication review yearbook* (Vol. 5, pp. 237–250). Beverly Hills CA: Sage.

Morley, D. (1986). *Family television: Cultural power and domestic leisure.* London: Comedia.

Morley, D. (1992). *Television, audiences & cultural studies*. London: Routledge.

Murdock, G., & Golding, P. (1977). Capitalism, communication and class relations. In J. Curran, M. Gurevitch, & J. Woollacott (Eds.), *Mass communication and society* (pp. 12–43). Beverly Hills, CA: Sage.

Neuman, W. R. (1982). Television and American culture: The mass medium and the pluralist audience. *Public Opinion Quarterly, 46,* 471–487.

Neuman, W. R. (1991). *The future of the mass audience.* Cambridge: Cambridge University Press.

Newcomb, H. M., & Alley, R. S. (1983). *The producer's medium.* New York: Oxford University Press.

Newcomb, H. M., & Hirsch, P. M. (1984). Television as a cultural forum: Implications for research. In W. Rowland & B. Watkins (Eds.), *Interpreting television* (pp. 58–73). Beverly Hills, CA: Sage.

Nielsen Media Research. (November, 1992). *DMA Test Market Profiles.* Northbrook, IL: Nielsen Media Research.

Nielsen Media Research. (1993). *1992–1993 Report on television.* New York: Author.

Nielsen Station Index. (February, 1986). *Viewers in profile.* Northbrook, IL: Nielsen Media Research.

Nielsen Television Index. (1988). *Program cumulative audiences: October 1988.* Northbrook, IL: Nielsen Media Research.

Niven, H. (1960). Who in the family selects the TV program? *Journalism Quarterly, 37,* 110–111.

Noam, E. (Ed.). (1985). *Video media competition: Regulation, economics, and technology.* New York: Columbia University Press.

Noelle-Neumann, E. (1973). Return to the concept of powerful mass media. In H Eguchi & K. Sata (Eds.), *Studies of broadcasting* (pp. 67–112). Tokyo: NHK.

Noelle-Neumann, E. (1984). *The spiral of silence.* Chicago: University of Chicago Press.

Noll, R. G., Peck, M. G., & McGowan, J. J. (1973). *Economic aspects of television regulation.* Washington, DC: Brookings Institution.

Ogburn, W. F. (1933). The influence of invention and discovery. In W.F. Ogburn (Ed.), *Recent social trends* (pp. 153–156). New York: McGraw-Hill.

Osborn, J. W., Driscoll, P., & Johnson, R. C. (1979). Prime time network television programming preemptions. *Journal of Broadcasting, 23*(4), 427–436.

Owen, B. M. (1975). *Economics and freedom of expression: Media structure and the first amendment.* Cambridge, MA: Ballinger.

Owen, B. M., Beebe, J. H., & Manning, W. G. (1974). *Television economics.* Lexington, MA: Lexington Books.

Owen, B. M., & Wildman, S. W. (1992). *Video Economics.* Cambridge: Harvard University Press.

Oxford English Dictionary (2nd ed.). (1989). New York: Oxford University Press.

Paik, J., & Marzban, C. (1995). Predicting television extreme viewers and non viewers: A neural network analysis. *Communication Research, 22,* 284–306.

Palmgreen P., & Rayburn, J. D. (1985). An expectancy-value approach to media gratifications. In K. E. Rosengren, L. A. Wenner, & P. Palmgreen (Eds.), *Media gratifications research* (pp. 61–72). Beverly Hills, CA: Sage.

Palmgreen, P., Wenner, L. A., & Rayburn, J. D. (1981). Gratification discrepancies and news program choice. *Communication Research, 8,* 451–478.

Palmgreen, P., Wenner, L. A., & Rosengren, K. E. (1985). Uses and gratifications research: The past ten years. In K. E. Rosengren, L. A. Wenner, & P. Palmgreen (Eds.), *Media gratifications research* (pp. 11–37). Beverly Hills, CA: Sage.

Pardun, C. J., & Krugman, D. M. (1994). How the architectural style of the home relates to family television viewing. *Journal of Broadcasting & Electronic Media, 38*(2), 145–162.

Park, R. E. (1970). *Potential impact of cable growth on television broadcasting* (R-587-FF). Santa Monica, CA: Rand Corporation.

Park, R. E. (1979). *Audience diversion due to cable television: Statistical analysis of new data* (R-2403-FCC). Santa Monica, CA: Rand Corporation.

Parkman, A. M. (1982). The effect of television station ownership on local news ratings. *Review of Economics and Statistics, 64*, 289–295.

Perse, E. M. (1986). Soap opera viewing patterns of college students and cultivation. *Journal of Broadcasting and Electronic Media, 30*, 175–193.

Perse, E. M. (1990). Audience selectivity and involvement in the newer media environment. *Communication Research, 17*, 675–697.

Perse, E. M., & Ferguson, D. A. (1993). The impact of the newer television technologies on television satisfaction. *Journalism Quarterly, 70*, 843–853.

Peterson, R. A. (1994). Measured markets and unknown audiences: Case studies from the production of culture and consumption of music. In J. S. Ettema & D. C. Whitney (Eds.), *Audiencemaking: How the media create the audience* (pp. 171–185). Thousand Oaks, CA: Sage.

Phalen, P. F. (1996). *Information and markets and the market for information: A study of the market for television audiences*. Unpublished doctoral dissertation, Northwestern University, Evanston, IL.

Philport, J. (1980). The psychology of viewer program evaluation. In *Proceedings of the 1980 technical conference on qualitative ratings*. Washington, DC: Corporation for Public Broadcasting.

Pietila, V. (1994). Perspectives on our past: Charting the histories of mass communication studies. *Critical Studies in Mass Communication, 11*, 346–361.

Poltrack, D. (1983). *Television marketing: Network, local, and cable*. New York: McGraw-Hill.

Porter, T. M. (1986). *The rise of statistical thinking: 1820–1900*. Princeton, NJ: Princeton University Press.

Radway, J. (1985). Interpretive communities and variable literacies: The functions of romance reading. In M. Gurevitch & M. R. Levy (Eds.), *Mass communication review yearbook* (Vol. 5, pp. 337–361). Beverly Hills, CA: Sage.

Rao, V. R. (1975). Taxonomy of television programs based on viewing behavior. *Journal of Marketing Research, 12*, 335–358.

Reagan, J. (1984). Effects of cable television on news use. *Journalism Quarterly, 61*, 317–324.

Red Lion Broadcasting Co., Inc v. FCC, 395 U. S. 367 (1969).

Robinson, J. (1972). Television's impact on everyday life: Some cross-national evidence. In E. A. Rubinstein, G. A. Comstock, & J. P. Murray (Eds.), *Television and social behavior: Vol. 4. Television in day-to-day life: Patterns of use* (pp. 410–431). Washington, DC: U.S. Government Printing Office.

Robinson, J. P. (1977). *How Americans used their time in 1965*. New York: Praeger.

Robinson, J. P., & Levy, M. R. (1986). *The main source: Learning from television news*. Beverly Hills, CA: Sage.

Rodriguez, A. (1996). Objectivity and ethnicity in the production of Noticiero Univision. *Critical Studies in Mass Communication, 13*, 59–81.

Rogers, E. M. (1994). *A history of communication study: A biographical approach*. New York: The Free Press.

Rosenberg, M. J., & Hovland, C. I. (1960). Cognitive, affective, and behavioral components of attitudes. In M. J. Rosenberg, C. I. Hovland, W. J. McGuire, R. P. Abelson, & J. W. Brehm (Eds.), *Attitude organization and change: An analysis of consistency among attitude components* (pp. 1–16). New Haven: Yale University Press.

Rosengren, K. E., Wenner, L. A., & Palmgreen, P. (Eds.). (1985). *Media gratifications research: Current perspectives*. Beverly Hills, CA: Sage.

Rothenberg, J. (1962). Consumer sovereignty and the economics of TV programming. *Studies in Public Communication, 4*, 23–36.

Rowland, W. (1983). *The politics of TV violence: Policy uses of communication research*. Beverly Hills, CA: Sage.

Rubin, A. M. (1984). Ritualized and instrumental television viewing. *Journal of Communication, 34*(3), 67–77.

Rubin, A. M. (1993). Audience activity and media use. *Communication Monographs, 60,* 98–115.

Rubin, A. M., & Perse, E. M. (1987). Audience activity and television news gratifications. *Communication Research, 14,* 58–84.

Rust, R. T. (1986). *Advertising media models: A practical guide*. Lexington, MA: Lexington Books.

Rust, R. T., & Alpert, M. I. (1984). An audience flow model of television viewing choice. *Marketing Science, 3*(2), 113–124.

Rust, R. T., & Donthu, N. (1988). A programming and positioning strategy for cable television networks. *Journal of Advertising, 17,* 6–13.

Rust, R. T., Kamakura, W. A., & Alpert, M. I. (1992). Viewer preference segmentation and viewing choice models of network television. *Journal of Advertising, 21*(1), 1–18.

Sabavala, D. J., & Morrison, D. G. (1977). A model of TV show loyalty. *Journal of Advertising Research, 17,* 35–43.

Sabavala, D. J., & Morrison, D. G. (1981). A nonstationary model of binary choice applied to media exposure. *Management Science, 27,* 637–657.

Salomon, G., & Cohen, A. (1978). On the meaning and validity of television viewing. *Human Communication Research, 4,* 265–270.

Salvaggio, J. L., & Bryant, J. (Eds.). (1989). *Media use in the information age: Emerging patterns of adoption and consumer use*. Hillsdale, NJ: Lawrence Erlbaum Associates.

Schmidt, B. C. (1978). Pluralistic programming and regulation for mass communications media. In G. Robinson (Ed.), *Communications for tomorrow* (pp. 191–228). New York: Praeger.

Schramm, W., Lyle, J., & Parker, E. B. (1961). *Television in the lives of our children*. Stanford, CA: Stanford University Press.

Schroder, K. (1987). Convergence of antagonistic traditions? The case of audience research. *European Journal of Communication, 2,* 7–31.

Schudson, M. (1984). *Advertising, the uneasy persuasion: Its dubious impact on American society*. New York: Basic Books.

Sears, D. O., & Freedman, J. L. (1967). Selective exposure to information: A critical review. In W. Schramm & D. Roberts (Eds.), *The process and effects of mass communication* (1971) (pp. 209–234). Urbana, IL: University of Illinois Press.

Sheperd, J. (1986). Music consumption and cultural self-identities: Some theoretical and methodological reflections. *Media, Culture and Society, 8,* 305–330.

Sherman, S. (1995). Determinants of repeat viewing to prime-time public television programming. *Journal of Broadcasting & Electronic Media, 39,* 472–481.

Signorielli, N. (1986). Selective television viewing: A limited possibility. *Journal of Communication, 36*(3), 64–76.

Sissors, J. Z., & Bumba, L. (1989). *Advertising media planning* (3rd ed.). Lincolnwood, IL: NTC Business Books.

Smythe, D. W. (1977). Communications: Blindspot of western Marxism. *Canadian Journal of Political and Social Theory, 1,* 1–27.

Smythe, D. W. (1981). *Dependancy road: Communications, capitalism, consciousness, and Canada*. Norwood, NJ: Ablex.

Soong, R. (1988). The statistical reliability of people meter ratings. *Journal of Advertising Research, 28,* 50–56.

Sparkes, V. (1983). Public perception of and reaction to multi-channel cable television service. *Journal of Broadcasting, 27,* 163–175.

Spaulding, J. W. (1963). 1928: Radio becomes a mass advertising medium. *Journal of Broadcasting, 7,* 31–44.

Spence, M. A., & Owen, B. M. (1977). Television programming, monopolistic competition and welfare. *Quarterly Journal of Economics, 91,* 103–126.

Spot Quotations and Data, Inc. (December, 1993). *SQAD Reports.* Elmsford, NY: Author.

Stanford, S. W. (1984). Predicting favorite TV program gratifications from general orientations. *Communication Research, 11,* 419–436.

Stanton, F. N. (1935). *Critique of present methods and a new plan for studying listening behavior.* Unpublished doctoral dissertation, The Ohio State University, Columbus, OH.

Steiner, G. A. (1963). *The people look at television.* New York: Alfred A. Knopf.

Steiner, G. A. (1966). The people look at commercials: A study of audience behavior. *Journal of Business, 39,* 272–304.

Steiner, P. O. (1952). Program patterns and preferences, and the workability of competition in radio broadcasting. *Quarterly Journal of Economics, 66,* 194–223.

Sterling, C. H., & Kittross, J. M. (1990). *Stay tuned: A concise history of American broadcasting* (2nd ed.). Belmont, CA: Wadsworth.

Sun, S. W., & Lull, J. (1986). The adolescent audience for music videos and why they watch. *Journal of Communication, 36*(1), 115–125.

Swanson, C. I. (1967). The frequency structure of television and magazines. *Journal of Advertising Research, 7,* 3–7.

Tannenbaum, P. H. (Ed.). (1981). *The entertainment functions of television.* Hillsdale, NJ: Lawrence Erlbaum Associates.

Tannenbaum, P. H. (1985). Play it again Sam: Repeated exposure to television programs. In D. Zillmann & J. Bryant (Eds.), *Selective exposure to communication* (pp. 225–241). Hillsdale, NJ: Lawrence Erlbaum Associates.

Television Bureau of Advertising. (1995). *Trends in television.* New York: Author.

Tiedge, J. T., & Ksobiech, K. J. (1986). The "lead-in" strategy for prime-time: Does it increase the audience? *Journal of Communication, 36*(3), 64–76.

Tiedge, J. T., & Ksobiech, K. J. (1987). Counterprogramming primetime network television. *Journal of Broadcasting & Electronic Media, 31,* 41–55.

Turow, J. (1984). Pressure groups and television entertainment: A framework for analysis. In W. D. Rowland & B. Watkins (Eds.), *Interpreting television: Current research perspectives* (pp. 142–162). Beverly Hills, CA: Sage.

Urban, C. D. (1984). Factors influencing media consumption: A survey of the literature. In B. M. Compaine (Ed.), *Understanding new media: Trends and issues in electronic distribution of information* (pp. 213–282). Cambridge, MA: Ballinger.

Veronis, Suhler & Associates. (1995). *Communications industry forecast.* New York: Author.

Vogel, H. L. (1994). *Entertainment industry economics: A guide for financial analysis* (3rd ed.) Cambridge: Cambridge University Press.

Wakshlag, J. J. (1977). *Programming strategies and television program popularity for children.* Unpublished doctoral dissertation, Michigan State University, East Lansing, MI.

Wakshlag, J., Agostino, D., Terry, H., Driscoll, P., & Ramsey, B. (1983). Television news viewing and network affiliation change. *Journal of Broadcasting, 27,* 53–68.

Wakshlag, J., & Greenberg, B. (1979). Programming strategies and the popularity of television programs for children. *Human Communication Research, 6,* 58–68.

Wakshlag, J., Vial, V. K., & Tamborini, R. (1983). Selecting crime drama and apprehension about crime. *Human Communication Research, 10,* 227–242.

Walker, J. R. (1988). Inheritance effects in the new media environment. *Journal of Broadcasting & Electronic Media, 32,* 391–401.

Walker, J. R., & Bellamy, R. V. (Eds.). (1993). *The remote control in the new age of television.* Westport, CT: Praeger.

Wand, B. (1968). Television viewing and family choice differences. *Public Opinion Quarterly*, *32*, 84–94.

Wartella, E. (in press). Audience effects research. In M. Cornfield, D. Gomery, & L. Lichty (Eds.), *A media studies primer*. Washington, DC: Woodrow Wilson Center.

Waterman, D. (1986). The failure of cultural programming on cable TV: An economic interpretation. *Journal of Communication, 36*(3), 92–107.

Waterman, D. (1992). "Narrowcasting" and "broadcasting" on nonbroadcast media: A program choice model. *Communication Research, 19*(1), 3–28.

Webster, J. G. (1980). *Factors mediating program preference as a determinant of television viewing behavior*. Unpublished doctoral dissertation, Indiana University, Bloomington, IN.

Webster, J. G. (1982). *The impact of cable and pay cable on local station audiences*. Washington, DC: National Association of Broadcasters.

Webster, J. G. (1983). The impact of cable and pay cable television on local station audiences. *Journal of Broadcasting, 27*, 119–126.

Webster, J. G. (1984). Cable television's impact on audience for local news. *Journalism Quarterly, 61*, 419–422.

Webster, J. G. (1985). Program audience duplication: A study of television inheritance effects. *Journal of Broadcasting & Electronic Media, 29*, 121–133.

Webster, J. G. (1986). Audience behavior in the new media environment. *Journal of Communication, 36*(3), 77–91.

Webster, J. G. (1989a). Assessing exposure to the new media. In J. Salvaggio & J. Bryant (Eds.), *Media use in the information age: Emerging patterns of adoption and consumer use* (pp. 3–19). Hillsdale, NJ: Lawrence Erlbaum Associates.

Webster, J. G. (1989b). Television audience behavior: Patterns of exposure in the new media environment. In J. Salvaggio & J. Bryant (Eds.) *Media use in the information age: Emerging patterns of adoption and consumer use* (pp. 197–216). Hillsdale, NJ: Lawrence Erlbaum Associates.

Webster, J. G. (1990). The role of audience ratings in communications policy. *Communications and the Law, 12*(2), 59–72.

Webster, J. G. (in press). Audience studies. In M. Cornfield, D. Gomery, & L. Lichty (Eds.), *A media studies primer*. Washington: Woodrow Wilson Center.

Webster, J. G., & Coscarelli, W. (1979). The relative appeal to children of adult versus children's television programming. *Journal of Broadcasting, 23*, 437–451.

Webster, J. G., & Lichty, L. W. (1991). *Ratings analysis: Theory and practice*. Hillsdale, NJ: Lawrence Erlbaum Associates.

Webster, J. G., & Newton, G. D. (1988). Structural determinants of the television news audience. *Journal of Broadcasting & Electronic Media, 32*, 381–389.

Webster, J. G., & Phalen, P. F. (1994). Victim, consumer, or commodity? Audience models in communication policy. In J. Ettema & D. C. Whitney (Eds.), *Audiencemaking: How the media create the audience* (pp. 19–37). Thousand Oaks, CA: Sage.

Webster, J. G., & Wakshlag, J. (1982). The impact of group viewing on patterns of television program choice. *Journal of Broadcasting, 26*, 445–455.

Webster, J. G., & Wakshlag, J. (1983). A theory of television program choice. *Communication Research, 10*, 430–446.

Webster, J. G., & Wakshlag, J. (1985). Measuring exposure to television. In D. Zillmann & J. Bryant (Eds.), *Selective exposure to communication* (pp. 35–62). Hillsdale, NJ: Lawrence Erlbaum Associates.

Webster, J. G., & Wang, T. Y. (1992). Structural determinants of exposure to television: The case of repeat viewing. *Journal of Broadcasting & Electronic Media, 36*(4), 125–136.

Weibull, L. (1985). Structural factors in gratifications research. In K. E. Rosengren, L. A. Wenner, & P. Palmgreen (Eds.), *Media gratifications research: Current perspectives* (pp. 123–148). Beverly Hills, CA: Sage.

Wells, W. D. (1969). The rise and fall of television program types. *Journal of Advertising Research, 9,* 21–27.

Wells, W. D. (1975). Psychographics: A critical review. *Journal of Marketing Research, 12,* 196–213.

White, K. J. (1977). Television market shares, station characteristics and viewer choice. *Communication Research, 4,* 415–434.

White, B. C., & Satterthwaite, N. D. (1989). *But first these messages... The selling of broadcast advertising.* Boston: Allyn and Bacon.

Why's and wherefore's of syndex II. (1988, May 23). *Broadcasting,* 58–59.

Wildman, S. (1994). One-way flows and the economics of audiencemaking. In J. Ettema & D. C. Whitney (Eds.), *Audiencemaking: How the media create the audience* (pp. 115–149). Thousand Oaks, CA: Sage.

Wildman, S. S., & Owen, B. M. (1985). Program competition, diversity, and multichannel bundling in the new video industry. In E. Noam (Ed.), *Video media competition: Regulation, economics, and technology* (pp. 244–273). New York: Columbia University Press.

Wildman, S. S., & Siwek, S. E. (1988). *International trade in films and television programs.* Cambridge, MA: Ballinger.

Williams, R. (1961). *Culture and society.* Hamondsworth: Penguin.

Williams, R. (1974). *Television: Technology and cultural form.* New York: Schocken Books.

Williams, F., Phillips, A., & Lum, P. (1985). Gratifications associated with new communication technologies. In K. Rosengren, L. Wenner, & P. Palmgren (Eds.), *Media gratifications research: Current perspectives.* (pp. 241–254) Beverly Hills, CA: Sage.

Wilson, C. C., & Gutierrez, F. (1985). *Minorities and media: Diversity and the end of mass communication.* Beverly Hills: Sage.

Wimmer, R. D., & Dominick, J. R. (1994). *Mass media research: An introduction* (4th ed.). Belmont, CA: Wadsworth.

Wirth, M. O., & Bloch, H. (1985). The broadcasters: The future role of local stations and the three networks. In E. Noam (Ed.), *Video media competition: Regulation, economics, and technology* (pp. 121–137). New York: Columbia University Press.

Wirth, M. O., & Wollert, J. A. (1984). The effects of market structure on local television news pricing. *Journal of Broadcasting, 28,* 215–224.

Wober, J. M. (1988). *The use and abuse of television: A social psychological analysis of the changing screen.* Hillsdale, NJ: Lawrence Erlbaum Associates.

Wober, J. M., & Gunter, B. (1986). Television audience research at Britain's Independent Broadcasting Authority, 1974–1984. *Journal of Broadcasting and Electronic Media, 30,* 15–31.

Wulfemeyer, K. T. (1983). The interests and preferences of audiences for local television news. *Journalism Quarterly, 60,* 323–328.

Zillmann, D., & Bryant, J. (Eds.). (1985). *Selective exposure to communication.* Hillsdale, NJ: Lawrence Erlbaum Associates.

Zillmann, D., Hezel, R. T., & Medoff, N. J. (1980). The effect of affective states on selective exposure to televised entertainment fare. *Journal of Applied Social Psychology, 10,* 323–339.

Author Index

Subject Index

155